# Landscape Written In His Face

# *Landscape Written In His Face*

*People, Places and Ideas in the Life and Work of*

# *Christopher Koch*

*Jamie Grant*

*Bonfire Monograph Series #1*

Published by Bonfire Books,
312 Queens Parade
Fitzroy North, VIC 3068, Australia
info@bonfirebooks.org
www.bonfirebooks.org



ISBN 978-1-7642190-3-7

A catalogue record for this book is available from the National Library of Australia

Cover: "Double-Humped Mount Direction" by Emily Grant

# *Contents*

# *INTRODUCTION*

Christopher John Koch was Australia's finest living writer of fiction. This description remained applicable, both in my opinion and in that of many others, from the publication of his first novel, *The Boys in the Island,* in 1958, until the appearance of his final work, *Lost Voices,* in 2012. Prize judges and ordinary readers alike shared my opinion, an opinion that was formed in response to those qualities of literary technique and writing style that seem to me essential in the assessment of any writer. Every Koch novel is distinguished by clarity of prose, a feeling for the rhythm and sound of sentences that might be expected from someone who began his writing career as a poet, a sure sense of form and structure, significant subject matter, strong characterisation, believable dialogue, and an underlying dimension that could be characterised as spiritual.

I was nine years old when *The Boys in the Island* was published, and sixteen when *Across the Sea Wall* first appeared; the only Australian fiction I was aware of by then were the children's novels of Frank Dalby Davidson, Nan Chauncy and Elyne Mitchell. Thus, the work of Koch was unfamiliar to me before the arrival of *The Year of Living Dangerously* on the international stage in 1978. After that, everyone knew him as C. J. Koch, prize-winning author of Australia's best-selling work of literary fiction, and script-writer for the Oscar-winning Peter Weir film. I met the author in 1980, and that led to a friendship propelled first by mutual interests in literature and a shared Tasmanian heritage, and later by my service as editor and proofreader for each novel from *Highways to a War* onward, while my wife, Margaret Connolly, acted as literary agent for those same novels.

The chapters which are to follow combine a certain amount of literary-critical scrutiny of the novels with an entwined series of recollections and descriptions of the personal interactions that produced them. Chris Koch, as I came to know him, was a man of many contradictions, not unlike some of the characters in his fiction, but at his best he was a delightful and highly amusing companion—yet this essay is not so much a biography as a loose set of biographical vignettes that revolve around the writing of each of his novels; it is an editorial or publishing history rather than a personal one. Chris did not want his biography to be written; only with some reluctance did he agree to Noel Hendricksen publishing his *Island and Otherland*, an academic thesis produced, improbably, by a pharmacist, and the suggestion that he write an autobiographical memoir himself was transformed early in the writing into the purely fictional *Lost Voices*.

A well-structured novel consists of a beginning, a middle and an end, and Koch understood the value of these elements as well as anyone. His novels begin, consistently, with a sentence that is unforgettable, then build through the middle toward a crisis that must be resolved; his endings leave the reader with a sense of the lives of his characters continuing beyond the time-scale portrayed in the novel. Koch also understood that a serious novel must deal with serious ideas and events, yet in dealing with some of the most momentous historic situations and political, philosophical and religious ideas of the past two centuries he was careful not to defend a single viewpoint, as different characters present both sides of any debate.

The characters in Koch's fiction are usually modelled on real people, and this is my justification for the biographical approach taken in these pages; it is helpful for the reader to know that, for example, the character of Mike Langdon in *Highways to a War* is based on the war photographer Neil Davis, or that of Robert Devereux in *Out of Ireland* on the real-life experiences of the Irish rebel John Mitchel, yet in the novels Langdon and Devereux soon develop lives of their own, transformed by the author's imagination. My intention, here, is to explain the workings of that imagination while placing it in the context of a selection of non-fictional instances.

The three (or four, if one includes the unpublished *The Dwarf of Melbourne*) novels that were completed before I made the acquaintance of their author are treated somewhat differently, but anyone who reads them will be struck, as I was, by the links between those early works and all that was to follow. Koch explicitly aimed to produce a single novel linked across two centuries in the form of the diptych *Beware of the Past*, which ultimately for practical reasons became two separate novels, and in his last novel, *Lost Voices*, he achieved his aim of a double narrative, with a book within the book. Yet it could be argued that his entire body of work is a single, interconnected fiction, not a diptych but a polyptych (if there is such a word), where themes, motifs, characters, events and places recur and echo one another over time.

*The Doubleman* was the last novel to list C.J. Koch as its author; *Highways to a War* is attributed to Christopher J. Koch, and the three novels that followed, *Out of Ireland*, *The Memory Room*, and *Lost Voices*, came from plain Christopher Koch. Likewise, in my long-standing association with him I at first addressed Koch as "Chris", but later as "Christopher" when it became evident that the unabbreviated version pleased him. This variation in nomination is mentioned here to explain the seeming inconsistency in the names employed throughout.

# *THE BOYS IN THE ISLAND*

In 1958, at the age of 26, Christopher Koch was at the beginning of what promised to be a lifetime of success. All that remained for him to decide was the exact direction of that success. He had been an artist, both professionally as a cartoonist for the Hobart *Mercury* and as a painter of watercolour landscapes, was a published poet whose work had attracted the admiration of such senior literary figures as Kenneth Slessor and Roland Robinson, had worked as a bookseller, before attending university, and then as a teacher, and as a labourer in order to save money for a trip through Asia to the United Kingdom. His experiences in Asia supplied such deep-rooted inspiration that four of his eight novels are set in Asian countries, from India and Indonesia to Vietnam, Cambodia and China. Yet it was in the United Kingdom that his future was decided, as he handed the completed manuscript of the book he had been working on since he was a university student, *The Boys in the Island,* to the literary agent Paul Scott, who was able to find a prestigious publisher for the novel in Hamish Hamilton Ltd, long before that imprint was swallowed by the Penguin conglomerate.

In 1958, it made sense for Koch to place his first novel with a British publisher. At the time the only significant Australian publisher was Angus & Robertson, noted for its list of verse, bush yarns and non-fiction rather than for serious literary novels. Most of the publishers active in Australia were branches of major British imprints, while smaller local publishers such as Lothian and

Georgian House survived as distributors of other British publishers (American publishers were forbidden by law from selling their books in the British Commonwealth). Thus, Koch began his publishing history as an international author, a fact which came to haunt him many years later, as British publishers became reluctant to take on authors from the Commonwealth without the right to distribute them world-wide. In 1958, Patrick White and Randolph Stow, who had recently published books with similar literary qualities to those of *The Boys in the Island,* both appeared with British imprints.

*The Boys in the Island* is often referred to as a promising apprentice work, a disguised coming-of-age autobiography, and yet when one reads the novel in the context of its author's later work, and when its prose style and technical structure are compared to those contemporary novels of White (*Voss* appeared in 1957) and Stow (*To the Islands*) and Hal Porter, one comes to realise that Koch had produced a mature and distinctive narrative that earned its place among the best of Australia's then-blossoming literature. As it was first published, that is, because it appeared with a major portion of the narrative excised: those passages concerning the character, Shane Noonan. They had been removed as a result of a legal threat from the family of the recently deceased, and notoriously litigious, businessman and criminal John Wren, who had sued over his portrayal in Frank Hardy's novel *Power Without Glory.* The suicide of Shane Noonan echoes the demise of Wren's son Tony, who had been a friend of Koch in university days. It should be added that John Wren's case against Frank Hardy failed, and Wren himself had died in 1953, so that Hamish Hamilton Ltd, perhaps because they were so far removed from Australia as to be unaware of that outcome, acted with notable cowardice. When *The Boys in the Island* came to be reprinted (by Angus & Robertson) in 1974 the excised passages were restored, to the benefit of the finished work.

*The Boys in the Island* is not a disguised autobiography, even though the author makes use of some of the elements of his early experiences. The central character, Francis Cullen, is described as follows: "He was an inoffensive yet very unsatisfactory boy in the eyes of the teachers, seeming to have no interest in anything that mattered, his attention to his work spasmodic and fleeting, coming only when something momentarily roused his interest." Cullen could be anyone or everyone, but he lacks the ambition and focus Koch himself must have possessed from an early age; all that he shares with the author is a sense that there is a life elsewhere, "a life lived inside a high, far melody, out in the wide-spread air." The novel's opening sentences bring to mind the opening of one of the pillars of Modernist literature, *A Portrait of the Artist as a Young Man*, by James Joyce, where a small child's viewpoint is captured by the onomatopoeia of language first heard but not fully understood: "The little boy stood looking at the Soons. *Soon! Soon! Soon!* They hummed: and it was not words the way people spoke words, it was a long humming song, going on and on. But he knew that it said *Soon*, and that he was meant to listen to it."

The echo of Joyce may have been one of the reasons for the early acclaim the novel received (there are similar echoes in the work of Stow), but when one reads it now what is most noticeable is its resemblance to the opening scenes of four of the subsequent seven novels that Koch published. This is a matter of resemblance, rather than of repetition: though Koch returns to similar settings and themes throughout his work, he does not repeat himself, and each novel can be seen as a unique literary achievement on its own. On the other hand, as one reads the novels in sequence there are so many scenes, images, ideas, characters and historical events which recur and overlap that it begins to feel as if they are all part of a single interconnected work. The connections begin early in *The Boys in the Island* when the young Francis Cullen "found himself in a little hidden lane, with a fence on one side and big clumps of fennel beside the railway embankment on the other. It was like a tunnel." This foreshadows the lane that haunts the opening pages of *The Doubleman* (1985), and continuing until *Lost Voices* (2012) where the narrator Hugh Dixon can be found standing "on the bridge I'd haunted as a boy. The train tracks were running as always between high, steep banks where the sun lay in dozing yellow patches, and ranks of wild fennel grew." In both of these passages, the impulse toward poetry can be seen in the rhymes (fennel and tunnel; banks and ranks) and rhythms of the sentences. The germ of the book in fact originated in a youthful set of poems.

Though *The Boys in the Island* includes many similar passages of poetry-infused landscape description, its success as a novel derives in the first instance from a powerful narrative drive, so that the reader feels impelled to turn the page to discover what is to happen next. This readability—which is a feature of all the novels Koch produced—is the characteristic that led certain critics to suggest that he was a mere commercial novelist, an author of "airport fiction." Yet no commercial fiction contains such depths of philosophical, political, emotional, spiritual and even geographical thought as do the novels of Koch; the fact that those ideas are set down in prose of such glass-clear clarity has deceived those critics who confuse density and obscurity of expression with depth.

In the first two chapters of *The Boys in the Island* there is only one boy, Francis Cullen, who is conscious that "He lived on an island. At six years old, after he had started school, Francis knew about that." In these simple sentences, and in all of the narrative of *The Boys in the Island*, lies the core of the unifying theme that is present throughout the literary output of Christopher Koch as much as it was present throughout his personal life. That theme could be described as double-sided, as it appears repeatedly in the novels as a lyrically expressed appreciation of the Tasmanian landscape, its hills and waterways and history-filled buildings, that nonetheless struggles against a yearning for an escape from that lyrical setting into a wider, less socially constricted world. Koch, in his lifetime, repeatedly left Tasmania to live in Melbourne, Asia, Europe, California, and a series of suburbs of Sydney and its outskirts, only to find himself in each new place deciding to return to the island of his birth—yet with each return he longed to escape again. In *The Doubleman* a smiling Franciscan preacher who visits the Catholic school attended by the narrator, Richard Miller, sums up the trajectory of this theme and of the author's life: *"We are like birds, we human beings: in the end we fly back to where we come from."*

In the third chapter of *The Boys in the Island* the boys become plural, as Francis Cullen becomes one of what he sees as "four lads". His yearning to escape is mixed with an urge to belong, to be a member of a group of his schoolmates. Then, in his last year at school, he forms a friendship with a boy called Lewis Mathews, a boy who "seemed to carry with him a secret life, elusive but hinted at in his face." Their friendship is "a joke not yet spoken by either of them. It did not need to be: it was the joke they had on school and the world, the casual yet important joke of their new friendship." Lewie, as he is known to his friends, or Bird, as he is nicknamed, is the first in a series of charismatic but flawed male characters who turn up in the lives of the plain, undistinguished but observant narrators and witnesses to the events in every Koch novel. At first the "sole ambition" of the new friends, though "ranging far, on the Mainland and beyond" is hardly what one would call ambitious: "'I can think of no better life,' Lewie had pronounced, gesturing largely, sprawled in the downtown milk-bar, 'than being a *bum*!'" Before their plans to range to the Mainland have advanced, Lewie invites Francis to join him and his friend Jake Brodie on a drive to a Carnival, "up the country, at Greendale", and soon Francis is "looking into the face of the girl the Carnival had promised him", a girl who "was pretty, although she was very small, with eyes as blue as hills", whose name is Heather Miles.

Heather, too, is a prototype for a series of similar female characters who appear throughout the novels, being first encountered in a country setting, like Deidre Dillon in *The Doubleman*, and seeming both alluring and unattainable, as are Deidre Dillon, Jill Bryant in *The Year of Living Dangerously*, and Maureen Maguire in *Highways to a War*. Ironically, the physical description of Heather Miles, Francis Cullen's first love, in the novel matches the appearance of Robin, Christopher's last love and second wife, even though Robin Whyte-Butler had only recently been born at the time *The Boys in the Island* was written; it was as if Koch had been searching all his life for the country girl "with vivid hill-blue eyes" he had conjured into existence as a young writer, or as if he had lived his life in reverse. Before Francis met Heather, the "vast fact of the Mainland sang in his head" but his passion for Heather puts that song to one side, even though her intimidating father does not like him, until after several summer months of train rides through the Tasmanian countryside she surprises him by announcing that she intends to marry a thuggish farm boy from the local area. As Francis rides the train home after this shock, "he whispered over and over to himself, in rhythm with the train: *So that was it. So that was it. So that was it.*" A moment of high emotion, once again, is expressed through onomatopoeia; it is followed almost at once by the discovery that Lewie, along with Jake Brodie, quite suddenly, had "left for the mainland."

In the final, unexpurgated version of the novel Francis does not immediately follow Lewie and Jake out of the island. Instead, on "a fine autumn day", he goes to the beach at Sandy Bay for a swim, and there, on "the hard sand at the water's edge", he recognises Shane Noonan, a boy who had been in his class in the final year of school, though they had not been friends. He did know that Shane had not been in Tasmania for long, that he came from a wealthy family, and that he had previously lived in Sydney. On the beach, Francis finds that "suddenly he wanted to get to know Shane Noonan" and starts to talk about "his plans for going to Melbourne in three months' time", to which Shane responds by looking "off across the estuary". "'You must look at those hills—' he pointed '—and wonder what's across there. There could be anything across there, because you've never left this island.'" From this conversation a friendship forms, and when Francis puts his plan of going to the Mainland into action it is because Shane is going there too.

Koch is justly regarded as an artistically masterful portrayer of Tasmania's landscapes and architecture (his great-grandfather was a noted colonial architect), but it is sometimes overlooked when his artistry is applied equally to other places. *The Boys in the Island* is as much a portrait of Melbourne in the 1950s as it is of Tasmania, just as *The Doubleman* brings the Sydney of the 1960s to life, and *The Memory Room* evokes Canberra. Francis and Shane arrive in "the bright-lit passenger lounge at Essendon, Melbourne's airport" together, but Shane immediately travels on to Sydney while Francis takes the bus to the "airways office" in the city, where Lewie and Jake are waiting to meet him, "standing in a light shower of rain on the wide Melbourne footpath". Riding in a cab "to the suburb called St Kilda", he looks out at "the city's shifting images: crossing and recrossing rails, gleaming in the rain, swing of headlight-stabbed roads, corner shops never before seen yet familiar as old dreams, huge lines and curves of unknown lights...a wide, straight highway of a size he had never seen."

If the city seems at first "bewildering and intoxicating", Francis soon has to face its reality, and the need to earn money to pay the rent on the single "shabby, high-ceilinged 19th century room" in a St Kilda boarding house that he shares with Lewie and Jake, so he begins to work "in an echoing concrete basement in one of the big buildings in Little Collins Street: a biscuit warehouse." Lewie, meanwhile, has taken his earlier ambition of "vagabondage" to a different level: he now aspires to become a criminal, and hopes to involve his room-mates in his schemes. Such an aspiration, one might feel, does not seem very sensible, but it has a propulsive effect on the narrative in the later chapters of the novel—after all, everyone likes to read crime stories. At first, this entails nothing more than shoplifting, in the company of a girl called Keeva, whose presence both allures and disturbs: "She was not good-looking, Francis thought; she was not even attractive. But her triangular face was disturbing, the skin seeming to be drawn taut from her chin by invisible cords. There was a life and a joking malice in her eyes unlike that of any girl Francis had met." Lewie, in particular, is "profoundly impressed by Keeva", and it is at her urging ("'But of course y' wouldn't have the guts,' she jeered") that he steals from the "cashbox" of the old man who lives in another room in the boarding house.

What follows is unexpected: a shape can be seen through the glass of "the French doors that led onto the room's little balcony." It is Shane Noonan. After several weeks, he has to admit, he "didn't make much of a success of Sydney." After a brief confrontation with Francis and Lewie, Shane walks out and Francis follows him, taking the train from St Kilda into the city. "Between the darkening cliffs of Bourke Street" Francis asks "'What *happened* in

Sydney?' '*Nothing* happened in Sydney,' Shane said. 'Do you understand, Francis? Nothing at all. Rather amusing that, isn't it? Except that I've realised a few things - what a fool I've been, and what a fool you are. *I've realized that nothing happens.* I wonder whether you've ever admitted that to yourself?'" Shane walks away again, and Francis follows until he "turned the corner and was out of sight." Hearing the sound of a disturbance around the corner, Francis investigates only to discover Shane in the process of being "taken in" by two policemen "for relieving himself in a public place". Three nights later some detectives come to the boarding house: Shane has committed suicide by throwing himself in front of a train at St Kilda station.

The death of Shane Noonan is the climax of the novel, though the narrative continues through a self-destructive drinking spree and a car-ride which ends in a fatal crash, and Francis waking up two weeks later "in his bed in Elimatta", the Hobart suburb where his parents live, knowing himself to be, as Shane had said, a fool. He has come back to Tasmania "to ask his father to send him back to school, to try again for his Leaving." Before this climax, Francis had "walked alone down to Marine Parade. It was a Sunday afternoon. He walked slowly, out of Fitzroy Street with its rattling palms and its small closed cafes, and along the wide promenade set with trim steel light-poles, beside the grey gleam of Port Phillip Bay." *Across the Sea Wall*, the second novel Koch was to publish seven years after the first, begins on Marine Parade, St Kilda, so that the two novels overlap despite a very different set of characters.

At the time of its publication, *The Boys in the Island* was universally praised, and its success led to Koch being offered the Stanford Writing Fellowship (also known as the Stegner Fellowship) in California, but its achievement has been somewhat eclipsed by the later novels even though a film version of the novel appeared in 1989. Admirers of

Koch should not neglect it, however. In its final form it is a complete and structurally perfect novel in its own right that nonetheless establishes the foundations for many of the themes and settings of the later works. It would not be unreasonable to regard the book, in that unhelpful marketing expression, as an Australian classic.

# *ACROSS THE SEA WALL*

For many writers, a second novel can be problematic. A successful debut might seem to invite a sequel, only for that sequel to face accusations of mere repetition; yet a novel that sets out in an entirely new direction can be seen as a betrayal of the author's original audience. Then there are critics who feel that the first novel was over-praised, who wait to bring the author back to earth in a harsh review of the second. By most standards, the reception of *Across the Sea Wall* was generous: it was praised by figures as significant as Kenneth Slessor and Anthony Burgess. Yet for Christopher Koch, one review, in the Melbourne *Age*, cancelled all the flattery and positive commentary that the book attracted. The author of the review was Neil Jillet, who was not even a regular literary critic: he was the film critic for *The Age*. For the rest of his life, Koch maintained a bitter animus toward Jillet, whom he would occasionally blame for the fourteen-year hiatus between his second and third published novels. This blame was unjustified, as we shall see.

*Across the Sea Wall* begins with a one-sentence paragraph: "He stood on Marine Parade." It ends, also, on the esplanade in St Kilda where some of the key passages in *The Boys in the Island* are located, but the main narrative takes place seven years earlier: on Marine Parade the thirty year-old Robert O'Brien looks back on the experiences of his twenty-three-year-old self and thinks "Part of me died here." Yet even though the settings overlap, the two novels could not be seen as related. O'Brien (who shares a surname with a fleeting character, Terry O'Brien, in the earlier of the two) is a completely different character to Francis Cullen, even though elements of both their stories are drawn from real-life events in the author's biography, and neither character resembles Christopher Koch himself. There is no yearning for the island landscapes of childhood in *Across the Sea Wall*, as O'Brien is a Sydney-based civil servant, with ambitions to become a journalist, who passes through Melbourne, initially, only to board the *Napoli*, a converted Italian freighter that will take him and his friend Jimmy Baden to Europe.

Though the novel is quite short—it is less than 150 pages—*Across the Sea Wall* is densely packed with incident, and with emotional tensions powerful enough to justify O'Brien's thought at the end, and its narrative architecture is solid and compelling. By any standard, it is a novel that can be appreciated on its own, aside from the context of the author's body of work. More significantly, however, the novel is the precursor, or prototype, for much of Koch's writing that was to follow. Most obviously, this comes from the Asian settings, as Koch was the first serious Australian novelist to take notice of the country's geographical neighbours. "At first landfall", the *Napoli* arrives in the Jakarta that will later become the backdrop for *The Year of Living Dangerously*. On board the ship, and more completely in Jakarta, O'Brien forms a connection with Ilsa Kalnins, a Latvian refugee or "New Australian" (a term she resents), a character type—the beautiful, precisely described woman with a foreign accent and an exotic yet tragic background—that is to recur in the form of Vera Chostiakov in *The Year of Living Dangerously*, and of Katrin Wilde in *The Doubleman*, and of Erika Lange in *The Memory Room*. These recurring female figures no doubt are derived in some way from Irene

Vilnonis, the first wife of Christopher Koch who was also the mother of his son, Gareth.

If the city of Jakarta, with its heat and poverty and the ubiquitous *betjaks* foreshadows the setting of a novel that is to come, another foretaste appears later in *Across the Sea Wall* amid a crowd of beggars on the streets of Madras: "And here was a legless dwarf, three feet high, in a white turban, with a large, dignified, almost intellectual face". Another ongoing theme in several of the novels makes its first appearance when O'Brien has a dream about "two little boys, in their beds", seeing "that they were men". "'Doubles', O'Brien said, and woke up saying it, with a start. 'Doubles.'" In *The Year of Living Dangerously,* Billy Kwan's files refer to doubles, and Guy Hamilton is seen as an improbable twin, in another anticipation of *The Doubleman*—then, later, in *Out of Ireland,* Robert Devereux admits "I am a man of double nature".

Another recurrent figure throughout the novels is a sinister yet charismatic and highly intelligent male character who has an unseen influence on the course of events: in *The Doubleman* this is Broderick, and in *Highways to a War* it is Aubrey Hardwick. Michael Maleter in *Across the Sea Wall* is the first of these characters to make an appearance. "I happen to be interested in existentialism", Michael says, and goes on to explain "We walk a tightrope with always the responsibility of choice on our heads"; O'Brien's response is "I still believe in good and evil", before Michael answers plausibly "it is rather a crude notion to say that nothing is good or bad for the existentialist." At the end of their conversation, O'Brien thinks "What bullshit he talks."

When he is first encountered his arguments seem persuasive even though he makes O'Brien feel uneasy, and at the novel's climax, when O'Brien catches a debilitating infection in Madras, it is Michael who saves him by moving him into a hotel room in Dalhousie, the "tiny, deserted hill-station left here by the British Raj like a discarded Edwardian toy." That he disappears having stolen O'Brien's traveller's cheques is a fitting conclusion.

For many years, the only critical response to *Across the Sea Wall* that seemed to influence Koch was that of Neil Jillet, and when the novel was reissued by Angus & Robertson in 1982 it had been substantially revised: "The cuts and alterations are not fundamental, but they are extensive", Koch wrote in an Author's Note. Most significantly, the narration was altered from first person to third person, and the Author's Note concluded with the hope that "the earlier version of this work will be consigned to oblivion". The first version of the novel had been completed while Koch was a fellow at Stanford University in California, being mentored by Frank O'Connor and enjoying the company of Ken Kesey and Larry McMurtry. Yet Koch had not been, despite his hints in later years, hurt into giving up on fiction in the fourteen years that passed between the unfavourable Jillet review and the triumphant publication of *The Year of Living Dangerously*. Seven years was the usual time-span it took for Koch to complete a novel, and by 1972 he had produced a manuscript with the title *The Dwarf of Melbourne*. Having finished it, though, he concluded that what he had written was not of a standard fit for publication, and resolved that this was another work that should be consigned to oblivion. For many years, it was presumed that the manuscript had been destroyed, but then it happened that Christopher asked me to come to Tasmania, where he was then living, to assist with preparing his literary papers for sale to the National Library (he understood, by then, that his cancer was terminal, and he hoped the papers might sell for about $5000, a useful sum for Robin in her approaching bereavement; in fact, they sold for more than ten times that amount). Opening a cupboard in the hallway, I saw a bound typescript with the title *The Dwarf of Melbourne,* but did not dare to read it in Christopher's presence. When I returned, later, the typescript was no longer there.

The dwarf of the title must have been an early version of Billy Kwan; Koch himself said as much, while admitting that the character of Billy Kwan was based on a friend of his from Melbourne days, John Quinlem, a Chinese-Australian who was not, however, a dwarf, despite sharing the intellect and the speech patterns given to Kwan. From Shane Noonan in *The Boys in the Island* onward, the major characters in all of the novels have their origins in real life—the experiences of R.J. Cook in *The Year of Living Dangerously* are those of Philip Koch, Christopher's brother. The reality-based vividness of the characters and the accurate depiction of real historic events that they are involved in contribute to the persuasiveness of the novels.

# *THE YEAR OF LIVING DANGEROUSLY*

For many writers, the opening sentence of a novel can be the key to its success (one thinks of the much-quoted first words of *Pride and Prejudice* or *Anna Karenina* or *Moby-Dick*), as a strong line can draw the casual reader into continuing. The first sentence of *The Year of Living Dangerously* consists of an unforgettable aphorism: "There is no way, unless you have unusual self-control, of disguising the expression on your face when you first meet a dwarf." With these words, Billy Kwan is introduced in the "permanent half-dark" of an air-conditioned hotel bar in Jakarta. It is "a foreigner's bar in a foreigner's hotel" where the "resident correspondents were drawn together—particularly the remaining English-speakers—in an artificially heightened good fellowship." This opening scene set in the bar introduces most of the novel's main characters by way of dialogue, while also introducing the essentials of the political situation in Indonesia that the correspondents are expected to cover. President Sukarno, who "gives each year a title", has announced the current one as "The Year of Living Dangerously".

The setting, in the bar, is hardly remarkable; there are similar scenes in many other novels. Yet Koch, in an extension of the obsessive sense of persecution that led him, earlier, to believe his career had been destroyed by Neil Jillet, became convinced that his idea had been stolen by the English spy writer John Le Carré for the opening scene of his novel *The Honourable Schoolboy.* Before it found a home with the English publisher Michael Joseph, the manuscript of *The Year of Living Dangerously* had been considered, and rejected, by a number of other publishers, and the reader for one of them happened to be John Le Carré's wife—or so Koch believed, in a story he told to his friends many times over. Having read *The Honourable Schoolboy,* one can only conclude that its opening scene, though set in the bar of the Foreign Correspondents' Club in Hong Kong, and including a dwarf among the characters drinking there, bears no more than a superficial resemblance to the Koch opening (the bar is thirteen floors up, rather than in a basement, while the dwarf is not even given a name, and speaks in a "queeny Greenwich Village drawl").

The success of his third novel can partly be attributed to a structural device Koch introduced to enhance the believability of the narrative: that is, the files of Billy Kwan. While the primary narrator of events in the novel is the journalist R.J. Cook (Koch is the German word for "cook"), Kwan becomes in effect a second narrator, whose viewpoint and opinions are quite unlike the first. In most of his subsequent novels Koch employs a similar device in order to suggest that what we are reading is an historical document rather than a fictional narrative: in *Highways to a War* this takes the form of the taped recollections of Mike Langford, as well as the interview transcripts from Harvey Drummond and Jim Feng; in *Out of Ireland* we are given to understand that the journal of Robert Devereux, along with a handful of letters to him, has been found inside the "mahogany writing slope" on the Langford family farm after Mike's death; in *The Memory Room* Vincent Austin keeps a diary.

The feature that set *The Year of Living Dangerously* apart, and led to it selling more paperback copies than any other Australian book up to its time, was the character of

Billy Kwan. In the gloom of the Wayang Bar he is first described as follows: "he was not really a dwarf in the extreme sense: that is, he was not a midget. His black, crew-cut head appeared large in relation to his body, and his legs were comically brief; but his chest and shoulders were powerful, and his hands square and capable-looking." The bar's name is a reference to the traditional Javanese shadow-theatre, the *wayang kulit*, and the plot of the novel echoes, but not does not trace too closely, one of the plays based on the great Hindu epic, the *Bhagavad Gita*, where the hero Arjuna joins with the dwarf Semar. The hero in this case is Guy Hamilton, the newly arrived correspondent for the ABS (the fictional version of the ABC both in this novel and in *The Doubleman* and *Highways to a War*), who arrives in the bar only to look "startled when he found himself confronted by Kwan." Hamilton is "a tall man in a well-cut tan suit", and beside Kwan his "tallness was fantastically exaggerated".

When Hamilton leaves the bar to "stretch his legs", Kwan insists on accompanying him, and as they go outside to where the "astounding heat of Java closed over them like a sack" it seems that Kwan is "eager to establish himself as guide, even as expert adviser." Then, as they go on, he begins to explain his own background: "'I wanted to be a secondary school teacher when I graduated,' Kwan said. 'I was young and innocent, then. Do you know what they said when they turned down my application? "Your appearance is against you."'" The same wording had been used by the Queensland Education Department to reject John Quinlem when he applied for a teaching position. "History's still my first love, old man; history and ideas", Kwan says before offering "his wide, frog-like smile." The history and ideas that interest Kwan are, of course, the interests of Koch, as such ideas are explored in increasing depth from this novel onwards. Importantly, Kwan's interpretations of events, and his political beliefs, as set out in his files, are very much the opposite of the author's: in most of the novels there are characters who argue the case, eloquently and sympathetically, for views that Koch does not agree with, as he leaves it up to the reader to decide whose ideas are right. Kwan's, clearly, are deluded, and they lead to his death, yet he is a highly attractive and interesting character, central to the plot.

Though *The Year of Living Dangerously* is a novel of the highest literary standard, with many passages of description that approach the quality of a poem, and political and philosophical discussions that have both depth and balance, while the characterisation even of minor figures is consistently memorable, it has also a plot that drives the narrative with the speed of a popular thriller. It is the sheer readability of Koch that has led some critics to mistakenly see him as a mere commercial thriller writer, in the genre of John Le Carré, his imagined enemy. Curiously, the readable qualities that became a pejorative in criticism of Koch, with the suggestion that all serious literature should be difficult to read, were overlooked toward the end of Le Carré's career, as he came to be regarded as a serious literary figure even though the characterisation, plotting and prose style in even the strongest of his works is wooden and simplistic when compared to Koch.

The plot of *The Year of Living Dangerously*, shadowing the *wayang* stories, seems to have been devised by Billy Kwan. When he first meets Hamilton in the bar, Great Wally, the twenty-two stone Australian journalist based on another real-life figure, the legendary Dick Hughes (in *The Honourable Schoolboy* the acknowledgements page mentions "the great Dick Hughes, whose outward character and mannerisms I have shamelessly exaggerated for the part of old Craw"), observes softly: "Billy's got himself a new hero." His other hero is President Sukarno, but there is little he can do to influence the

President's life; instead, he takes it upon himself to shape Hamilton's career and even his love life. Hamilton's ambition, a humble one, is to do well enough in his new position to avoid being sent by his employer back to the news-room: "The news-room's a graveyard," he says. "A bloody graveyard." At the same time he is unmarried, so that "All this made him the perfect vessel for Billy Kwan's purposes."

Those purposes take Hamilton, with the use of Kwan's contacts and local knowledge, to the centre of the murky political situation in Jakarta, and he soon receives a congratulatory telegram from his news-editor—"we called them 'herograms' in the Wayang". (After the novel had been published, Koch discovered the word "herogram" in *The Honourable Schoolboy,* and saw it as further proof that his manuscript had been stolen). Then Kwan introduces him to Jill Bryant, "a secretary at the British Embassy. Jill's a nice little thing - I'd like you to meet her." Among the dossiers and diary entries in Kwan's filing system, he writes "*here, among my files, I can shuffle like cards the lives I deal with.*" He has decided to bring Jill and Guy together: "You two are made for each other", he says, before making an "offer whose motives Hamilton found difficult to fathom." "Look, if you want to get away from everyone there's always my bungalow. I'm often out, and I'll lend you the key." When they take up the offer they find that, "rather oddly and inconveniently", the door to the bathroom is locked. Two days later, Hamilton returns to the bungalow to find that one of the files in the "grey steel cabinet" has been left out: it is headed *DOSSIER B 26: BRYANT, Gillian Edith*. Having made this discovery, and read the contents of the file, which includes nude photographs of Jill ("he was, after all, a brilliant photographer") Guy discusses what he has seen with the sympathetic "Cookie": "'The idea of dossiers being kept on people gives me the creeps, anyway; but when a private person does it—' He searched for words. 'The little bastard's playing God,' he said."

If Kwan is playing God, he is not quite as all-powerful as he might like to be. While Jill is in Singapore, Guy agrees to go for "a simple week-end in the hills" with his Indonesian assistant (and suspected Communist Party operative) Kumar, yet as they are leaving Kumar suddenly announces "We have a passenger in the car, boss, I hope you don't mind. Her name is Vera Chostiakov. She is attached to the Soviet Embassy." Soon the Russian girl has "aroused both his curiosity and his lust", to Kwan's disapproval: "If I were you, old man, I'd keep well away from her." This warning is expanded in the file Kwan keeps on Hamilton: "*I sense the invasion of Durga's darkness in you: she who turns time into sleep, and love into lust, and life into death*". The temptation is offered to Guy in the context of a potentially sensational rumour, for his journalistic career, about a shipment of arms from the Communist Chinese government to the Indonesian communists, the PKI. Another entry in Kwan's files addresses Guy about this matter: "*You are apparently too stupid - or too vain - to have realised what the lady wants from you: the details and date of arrival of the Chinese arms shipment.*"

Spitefully, Kwan informs Jill that Guy has "betrayed" her, and from this point the narrative accelerates toward its dramatic, and tragic, conclusion. The tragedy is that both of Billy Kwan and of Indonesia as a nation, where the political circumstances described in the novel eerily anticipate the politics of the present day, sixty years after the event, where charismatic leaders, presenting themselves as saviours, are elected on the basis of vainglorious, or utopian, promises that cannot be fulfilled in reality. Bitter disillusionment with those leaders follows not long after each election. Thus Billy Kwan, who had worshipped Sukarno, makes one of his final file entries an accusation of his former hero, "Bung Karno": "*He builds his futile monuments, instead of drains which would rid the city of disease! He starves and kills, with his egomaniac foolishness, the children of his people.*"

*The Year of Living Dangerously* combines the fast-moving narrative of a political thriller with a complex love story, fraught with obstacles, all set against a background of Javanese culture, Hindu mythology and revolutionary theory (there are also extended reflections, in Kwan's writings, on the physiology of dwarfism and the place of dwarfs in culture and history across the world). All of these elements combine to produce an irresistible best-seller, a novel that won major prizes, and became the basis for an Oscar-winning movie. Yet when the novel burst into public view I had not read anything written by C.J. Koch, as he was then known, and had only heard his name through a chance conversation with Les Murray three years before its publication.

In 1976 Les Murray, who I knew as the acting editor of the magazine *Poetry Australia*, came to Melbourne, where I lived at the time, to collect the first prize in what was then the richest poetry prize in Australia, sponsored by the Victorian government. Before the prize-giving ceremony in the Treasury building, Les got me to meet him in a coffee shop near his cheap hotel. "I don't want to be like my mate Koch," he told me, before relating the experience of this, to me, unknown person called Koch who had come to Melbourne to accept a literary prize (it was in fact the Stanford writing scholarship) only to fall into the wrong company. A group of friends took him on a pub crawl that left him so befuddled that when the time came for him to take a taxi to the Hawthorn mansion of the society lady who was patron of the prize he could do no more than slur the word "Haaaawthorn" to the driver, being discovered later asleep in the master bedroom in the midst of the reception in his honour. In Murray's poem

"The Quality of Sprawl" there is a reference to this incident, with Christopher's name changed to Calum:

> Sprawl is really classless, though. It's John Christopher
>         Frederick Murray
> asleep in his neighbour's best bed in spurs and oilskins
> but not having thrown up:
> sprawl is never Calum who, in the loud hallway of our
>         house,
> reinvented the Festoon...

At the time, it seemed to me that Koch was simply a figure of legend, who had not produced any form of writing for more than a dozen years. Then *The Year of Living Dangerously* appeared.

Early in the year 1980 I agreed to drive my friend Roger McDonald from Melbourne to Adelaide, where he was to be awarded the biennial Writers Week prize for his novel *1915*. My brother Pat, who was then representing Roger's publisher, University of Queensland Press, was in the car as well. The prize was presented to Roger at a winery outside Adelaide; under the vines, someone introduced me to Chris Koch, a dark-haired man of average height with a glint of humour about his eyes and a mouth that seemed about to break into a smile. "I know about you," I told him. "I am a friend of Les Murray." "Any friend of Les is a friend of mine," he replied. We arranged to have dinner later in the week and found, over an Italian meal in Hindley Street, that we had much in common, planning to meet again on my next visit to Hobart, a visit that was not to be. By this time, I had read *The Year of Living Dangerously* and could understand the acclaim it had attracted: the book itself was in the process of being transformed into a film by Peter Weir. Chris did not enjoy this process, and disliked Weir to the point that he asked for his own name to be removed from the film's credits, but on the set he met a production assistant called Cynthia Blanche who moved in with him after his marriage to Irene broke up, and he moved from Hobart to Neutral Bay in Sydney, escaping the island once again.

# *THE DOUBLEMAN*

Chris and Cynthia had moved from a flat in Neutral Bay to a house in Turramurra by the time I had the opportunity to read his new novel, *The Doubleman*, in manuscript form. Chris showed it to me, with the reluctant permission of his new literary agent (Paul Scott having long since died), Tim Curnow of Curtis Brown Australia, and of John Cody, the Australian representative of his new English publisher, Chatto and Windus, so that I could select an excerpt suitable for publication in *The Age Monthly Review*, the Melbourne newspaper that Robert Gray and I were editing a fiction and poetry supplement for. I chose the opening scene, and it was given the title "The Man in the Lane", and the excerpt went on to win a prize that was briefly inaugurated for the best piece of writing published in our supplement. The Turramurra house, built into the side of a hill, had a separate apartment underneath the main living quarters, where Gareth Koch was able to live independently. The front door opened directly into Christopher's study, a book-lined space of spotless, library-standard orderliness with a tidy desk in one corner.

The man in the lane, in that opening scene, disappears mysteriously after a brief conversation in which he advises the narrator, a Catholic schoolboy called Richard Miller, to change his school: "The Brothers are hard men," he says softly. Several years later he reappears outside a second-hand shop where Miller's cousin Brian Brady is fascinated by a guitar in the "dusty display window" and doesn't "seem to have changed or aged". His surname, it emerges, is Broderick, though his first name remains unrevealed for a long time, and he is both the accountant and buyer for the shop (and possibly its real owner) as well as being a skilled guitarist and guitar teacher. He may be the "Doubleman" of the novel's title, or this may be Darcy Burr, the nephew of Sandy Lovejoy, the shop's nominal owner. Broderick leads the two young cousins into the shop and picks up the guitar to play "a flamenco piece": "He didn't play very fast, and yet the delicate, tripping, fandango sound seemed to be fast, like a dance. The strange broken gypsy rhythms and the halts and changes of direction kept us in a state of tension, half pleasurable and half not. The rhythm was compulsive, making us tap our feet; and the music should have been gay. Yet it wasn't quite gay; there was an opposite seriousness and perhaps despair under it, throbbing in the bass strings."

This brilliant and precisely detailed description of a flamenco guitarist at work is a portrait of Gareth Koch in performance, even though at the time it was written Gareth was still a student. He was to become a distinguished flamenco guitarist and a university music teacher. The key to Broderick, however, can be found in a book Chris encouraged me to read soon after *The Doubleman* was published, *The Private Memoirs and Confessions of a Justified Sinner*, by James Hogg, written in 1824. In Hogg's book, there is a persuasive "young gentleman" who has the "chameleon art" of changing his appearance, who turns out to be the Devil, and whose aim is to convince a young Calvinist believer that all his crimes are justified by Calvin's doctrine of predestination. As with Broderick, the young gentleman's name remains unknown for most of the novel; the man in the lane's comment about "the Brothers" suggests, without stating it directly, that he is an enemy of the Catholic church (Hogg's novel is a satirical polemic by a Catholic against the Scottish

Protestants). The climax, and the resolution, of *The Doubleman* comes when Richard Miller goes into the Catholic church in Roslyn Gardens, near Kings Cross, where "Evening Mass was beginning".

Until this moment, Miller has been what we would call a "lapsed Catholic", but the religious themes of temptation, mystery and redemption are buried beneath the structure of this fast-moving, highly contemporary novel. The opening chapters return to the setting of *The Boys in the Island*, after two novels set on the mainland and in Asia. Miller's childhood experiences, his suburban Hobart surroundings, his Catholic schooling, and his sense that there is another, larger world beyond the confines of the island all resemble the early experiences of Francis Cullen: "I'm entranced for an hour at a time by Mount Direction: a mauve, double-humped hill lying to the east. No one, I believe, has ever loved a hill or a mountain as I do; Mount Direction is not just a mountain; it's the sign of an amazing Beyond." "Double-humped Mount Direction" recurs as a description in several places in the novels that are to follow, as do Catholic childhoods and the Hobart suburbs. Yet Richard Miller, like Francis Cullen, is not a self-portrait by the author, as in each case there are important points of difference with the early years of Christopher Koch. In the case of Miller, it is "the mask of paralysis", the polio infection that strikes him down in early childhood, leaving him with a crippled left leg and "consequences less obvious": "It was now that my interest in the Otherworld began."

Koch never suffered from polio, nor did he endure the asthma that afflicts Robert Devereux in *Out of Ireland*, as he was a healthy and vigorous individual for most of his long life. Despite this, one of the most powerful features of the fictional worlds that he was to create is the precise depiction of illness, its symptoms and its psychological effects, whether it be polio, asthma, or the tropical fevers suffered in Asia. The "interest in the Otherworld" turns out to be more significant than the effects of "crippledom", however, "that Otherworld of mauve mists and round, enchanted hills: Elfland!" Discouraged by his mother from reading "novels for adults" by the likes of Dickens and Scott ("she had, in fact, an Irish Catholic suspicion of most books, since sexual passion and terrible nudities were liable to be sidling about in them"), Miller as a boy turns to books "devoted to fairies, and figures of legend". These legends, as the novel comes to show, contain messages that are the opposite of Christian beliefs.

When Miller's convalescence is over, the last sign of his affliction a withered left leg, so that he knows that he will "never run fast again", he becomes close at school to his cousin Brian Brady, son of his mother's brother Mick Brady. Like Mike Langford in *Highways to a War*, Brady is descended from an Irish convict transported to Van Diemen's Land in 1848. At first, he seems to occupy a similar position in Miller's life to that of Lewis Mathews in the life of Francis Cullen in *The Boys in the Island*, but the relationship becomes more complex as Brady discovers an interest in music and begins to take lessons from Broderick. In a "quiet, almost monotonous voice" Broderick says at the end of one lesson "No real mystery can be solved... like those mysteries of religion your Church talks about", before going on to add "Eventually you may discover mysteries that are less boring."

Perhaps prompted by Broderick's talk, Brady assaults Brother Kinsella, the hardest of the hard men who teach at St Augustine's, when the brother tries to confiscate his guitar "two weeks from the end of the final term". He then persuades his cousin to join him on a two-day bicycle ride to his parents' farm near Swansea, on Tasmania's East coast. The rural setting, and the events that take place there, echoes the central scene of *The Boys in the Island*, where Francis Cullen falls in love with Heather Miles, yet

Richard Miller's meeting with Deidre Dillon, a "paying guest" at Greystones, the Brady family farm where "a significant part of the farm's income" comes from its role as an "unofficial guest house", leads to further complications. These complications are hinted at in the epigraph to the chapter "Mrs Dillon", a quotation from the Scottish ballad "Tam Lin": "When we were frae the hunting come, / That frae my horse I fell; / The Queen o Fairies she caught me, / In yon green hill to dwell." The Queen of Fairies is an unhappily married woman, not much older than the eighteen-year-old Richard, who lives in Sydney and tempts him to come and join her when the holiday at the farm is at an end. At the same time, Brian Brady has become involved with his family's "hired help", Hazel Pearce, and as a result has "left home for good, riding his bicycle back down the highway to Hobart" after a quarrel with his father. It is the beginning of his career as a musician.

Eighteen months later, when Miller is an Arts/Law student at university as well as an amateur actor in his spare time, he encounters Brady with Darcy Burr in a "seedy, out-of-the-way pub" where he had gone on one of his "periodic drinking bouts". Drinking to excess is another common theme in the novels from *The Boys in the Island* onward, and as Les Murray's anecdote suggests (and a passage in *The Many-Coloured Land* confirms) it was also a feature of Christopher's early life. In the pub, Miller goes into the lounge to listen to the music "produced by a skinny old lady in a hat, who played the piano": "As she finished, the frosted-glass doors to the hallway opened and two young men came in, carrying guitar cases." Unseen by them as their performance begins, Miller is "startled at their technical virtuosity". Reunited with Brady and Burr, Miller soon learns that they too have developed an interest in the Otherworld. At a seance it seems they have made contact with the spirit of Hazel Pearce, who turns out to have died after having an abortion (a "back-alley job in

Launceston") not long after Brady's quarrel with his father. When Miller expresses disgust with the seance, Burr explains "Brod taught us about the spirits...and a lot of things beside the guitar. We went to a different university from you, Dick."

Even though he feels that "there was something vaguely threatening about him at times", Miller finds Burr persuasive enough to follow his advice and drop out of university, going to work in the shop with Broderick. His real ambition is "to go to drama school in Sydney and to survive there as an actor"—this ambition has a "double edge", "since to reach Sydney, I thought, would reunite me with Deidre." First, he has a conversation with Broderick in his "narrow, windowless office" about the philosophy he had been studying at university, which turns to the Christian religion: "I can't take Christianity very seriously, I'm afraid," Broderick says, before shocking Miller despite his "agnosticism": "Christ was a clown...he died a clown's death." Even an agnostic is "uncomfortable at hearing Christ mocked." Later, Darcy Burr says to him: "Brod's got powers", and Dick, as Darcy addresses him (the character's name, in the novel, may have been derived from that of Dick Connolly, a colleague and close friend of Chris Koch when they both worked at the ABC), wonders what those powers might be. "Brod can travel", Darcy says. "Brod's been seen in one place, while his real self's in another."

Abruptly, Brady and Burr disappear. They have, it seems, gone to Sydney to pursue their musical ambitions. Yet Miller is unable to follow them, as he has just received a letter from Deidre Dillon telling him "You have to forget me." Instead, like Francis Cullen in *The Boys in the Island*, he moves to Melbourne, where seven years pass during which he works as an actor while his "hopes of a big career in the theatre" fade. Instead, he realises that he "wanted to direct actors", not to be one, and that he would prefer to do so on "the handsome salary paid to a producer in ABS, the national broadcasting service". An "imminent vacancy at Head Office in Sydney" lures him to "depart this flat city on the southernmost edge of the continent and to take flight north to the unknown metropolis of sun."

What follows is an evocation of Sydney in the 1960s, its climate and its culture, the architecture and the glittering harbour, and the run-down Bohemia of Kings Cross, where Miller finds a room in a boarding house, that is every bit as vivid and detailed as the evocation of the Tasmanian landscape earlier in the novel. Before he manages to obtain a job with the broadcasting service (as Christopher Koch had done in the late 1950s), Miller meets Katrin Vilde, another one of the tenants in his boarding house—and another version of Christopher's first wife. Katrin is a refugee from Estonia, who becomes Miller's wife; she is also a gifted singer, and when Darcy Burr surprisingly reappears in Miller's life her voice becomes the key to the success of the popular folk- singing group "The Rymers" that Burr and Brian Brady have begun. With Miller as their producer, the group are soon acclaimed for their recordings, and for an ABS television series. The group's popularity (which is compared in the novel to that of the real-life group The Seekers, who were clearly a model for the fictional creation) derives not only from Katrin's singing but also from the melodies and the subjects that their songs are based on, the "English and Scots ballads of the supernatural".

The exact meaning of the supernatural, its sinister implications, begins to emerge as the group progresses from one success to another. When Miller and his cousin Brian Brady are first reunited in the Hasty Tasty, a King's Cross cafe that serves "terrible grey coffee", one of his first questions is "What became of Broderick?" "'Brod?' Brian says. 'That was a bit queer. Brod disappeared.' 'Disappeared? How?' 'He vanished about five years ago... No one knew where Brod went, or why; he didn't tell them at the bookshop he was leaving.'" Burr has told Brady that Broderick is dead, but he also seems to believe that he can communicate with him, as in the seances they had conducted years before; and Burr, with his belief in the "Faery Otherworld" is the driving force behind the Rymers. "Lying back in an armchair", smoking a damp marijuana joint, "'Fairyland's double,' Darcy said." The expression brings to Miller's mind a remark of Broderick's, "something about the universe itself being double." Then Deidre Dillon also reappears. Even though she knows that Miller is married, she tries to lure him back into her "fairyland", as well as getting her stepson Patrick a place as a drummer with the Rymers.

Darcy Burr's ambitions for the group collapse when Miller, who is effectively their manager, Brady and Katrin refuse to undertake a tour of Britain and Europe, partly because they do not like the way that he has "these little teenage girls coming in and out all the time... Darcy gives them pot", and partly because, Brian says, "I never liked this fairy stuff you and Darcy cooked up." Deidre is killed by her stepson, in what may or may not have been an accident in their house at Palm Beach, and Patrick drives Miller "up the Barrenjoey Road in his red MG". At the house, Miller "realised that someone was looking at me, standing by the aloe at the top of the sandstone steps. It was Clive Broderick... His head was cocked, and his winter-blue eyes held a quizzing expectancy. He would always wait; he would wait through eternity." Then he sees that the figure is that of Darcy Burr. To the reader, the possibility occurs that Burr and Broderick are the same, though this is never stated in the novel.

*The Doubleman* shows how belief in those stories of the supernatural that oppose Christianity, and the use of artificial stimulants such as drink, drugs and "Darcy's magic mushrooms", lead to depravity and murder, yet it also portrays convincingly the self-contained worlds of music and broadcasting, while telling a story that compels from the first page to the last. The novel justly won the Miles Franklin Award and was shortlisted for other prizes and highly praised by reviewers—with one exception. By the time the novel was about to be published, I had decided, like Richard Miller, to leave Melbourne, the "flat city on the southernmost edge of the continent" to move to the "metropolis of the sun". At first, there was temporary accommodation for me in the house of the poet Geoffrey Lehmann, who regarded himself as a "novel doctor" and was reading *The Doubleman* in manuscript form. Geoff's advice to Chris was that he should cut the scene in Chapter 7 where the group meets the international talent scout Roy Slade, and Chris took this suggestion to heart; only after the book was in print did he realise that the ending did not quite make sense without that scene, which was restored in later printings.

I had settled in Sydney, in my cousin's house in Leichhardt, at the end of July 1984; from that time forward I met frequently with Chris Koch, either in cafes and restaurants in the city, or at the house in Turramurra. By October I had moved into a flat in Lilyfield, and in that month I arrived for one of the dinner parties that Chris loved to hold, to find Les and Valerie Murray, along with the colourful Piers Laverty, Les Murray's satellite, waiting in the living room. The phone began to ring, and Chris rushed to answer it: "He's got another girlfriend," Cynthia smiled, "and he thinks I don't know." We moved to the dining room, and Chris asked, "Are you hungry, Les?" Before the corpulent Les could answer, Piers drawled "Are the Kennedys gun-shy?" Later that night, as Les drove me back to Lilyfield, he observed "I'm worried about Christopher. He did not seem unhappy to see the back of us." This was the first sign, to me, of a falling-out between the two of them, after Les had been one his longest-standing friends in Sydney, and one of his most influential supporters. A few days later, Chris asked me to meet him for lunch in the city, where he explained that in his opinion Murray's egotism was getting out of hand. "Australians don't like a boaster," he said.

Despite this, Les and Chris were meeting regularly at this time, often at the Capitan Torres restaurant in the city, a dark-panelled, garlic-scented Spanish establishment that reminded Chris of the time he had spent in Madrid where Gareth first became interested in the flamenco guitar; apart from me and Les, the group of Koch cronies who gathered at the Capitan Torres included Robert Gray, Tim Bowden, Gary Scarrabellotti, and the man Chris called "the world's most conservative journalist", Greg Sheridan. There were also dinners, morning teas and barbecues at the house in Turramurra, which was where several of us had gathered soon after the publication of *The Doubleman.* The reviews had begun to appear, all of them favourable except for a notice in *The National Times* (a newspaper that is now long defunct) by Sydney University's Don Anderson—this notice, too, was largely favourable, but it concluded with one minor reservation (I can no longer recall what the reservation was) intended to show that the academic reviewer had not been taken in. For Chris, this was "a knife job", and he bewailed the ruin of his career to me and Les, who knew how to console him: "He's shot out one of your tyres, but you're driving a six-wheeler."

*The National Times,* in those days, published a weekly literary gossip column written by Tom Thompson, an aspiring but not very promising writer who would go on years later to achieve a form of celebrity as the subject of an Archibald Prize winning portrait. For two weeks out of three in the month of May his column had included snide references to me (I had a certain notoriety at the time, as the author of a regular column in *The Age Monthly Review*), but the second snide remark was made in the context of a flattering comment about Chris Koch. The three of us were in the bar at the Capitan Torres when this was pointed out; Les said immediately, "Christopher, you are swimming to safety through the blood of your friends." A month later I had dinner with Chris at the Torres; Robert Gray was supposed to join us, but even though he did appear briefly, he soon made an excuse and left. Before we ate, Chris told me that he and Cynthia had broken up. Then, after dinner, Chris decided that we should have a coffee somewhere else, and we walked around the corner to Park Street where there was an old-fashioned cafe not unlike the Hasty Tasty in *The Doubleman*. At one of the tables there was an elderly man with a hooked nose and penetrating eyes, sitting with a beautiful young girl who might have been his daughter (it was his wife): he greeted Chris and insisted that we join them. The elderly man turned out to be a folk singer called Alex Hood, who reminded me of one of the characters in the novel.

Two months later, Geoff Lehmann and Chris Koch were no longer "on speaking terms", as Geoff took Cynthia's part in the break-up. *The Doubleman* won the Miles Franklin Award, and it was on the short list for the New South Wales Premier's Prize, judged by, among others, Les Murray. When the Premier's Prize for fiction went to someone else, Chris was furious at what he saw as a "betrayal" by Les. In fact, Les had argued passionately on the committee in favour of Chris for the prize, but he had put himself in a difficult position; he had also argued passionately for Kevin Hart, his protege, to be given the poetry prize for his book *Your Shadow* even though the Hart book had been published in the wrong year. The other committee members told Les that he could have one of the books he favoured as a winner, but not both, and Les chose Kevin Hart. Though this was explained to Chris, he did not believe it, and this presumed betrayal became another step on the long disillusionment with Les that became a lasting estrangement.

That disillusionment had begun five years earlier, when Les published his verse novel *The Boys who Stole the Funeral*—Chris felt that, as a poet, Les had no business venturing into the novelist's narrative territory (the title of the Murray book was an echo of *The Boys in the Island*), and even Les was aware of the issue, as on presenting a copy of the book to Chris he added the following inscription: "for Chris, This naughty incursion into the novelist's patch! With love from Les." Exactly twelve months after Chris had told me about his break-up with Cynthia, he introduced me to his new girlfriend, Adrienne Jones. Soon after this, Chris sold the house in Turramurra: he told me that he and Adrienne had decided to move to Bilgola Plateau after meeting the ABC television personality Iain Finlay, whose house on the plateau was for sale at a very reasonable price, and that he was beginning to feel exhausted with the steep uphill walk to Turramurra station.

The house at Bilgola had magnificent views over the ocean, and a glimpse of the patch of sub-tropical vegetation that had been used in the film of *The Year of Living Dangerously* to represent the Indonesian jungle; the house also had a mirror on the bedroom ceiling, and an open plan layout that did not quite suit Chris when he came to create his study. The climb from the nearest bus stop was even steeper than the hill at Turramurra. The dinner parties and lunches resumed, but those of us who were invited had further to travel, while Chris himself travelled extensively in the years after *The Doubleman* appeared, including a trip to New York, where he met Adrienne, a Literature Board-sponsored trip to China with Nicholas Hasluck, and a week in India with Les Murray, despite their falling out. While living at Bilgola he also published the essay collection *Crossing the Gap*. This book appeared only because its author had conceived an intense dislike of Carmen Callil, the Australian-born head of Chatto and Windus, and of Chatto's local representative John Cody.

Chris was determined that his next novel should not be published by Chatto, but his agent, Tim Curnow, had signed him to a two-book deal that obliged him to show them his next work. Chris reasoned that, in the current climate, no publisher would wish to consider a collection of essays, so that he could be released from his contract if he offered a collection of essays to Chatto and had it rejected. This scheme did not work as he had intended: Carmen Callil, unaware of his dislike of her, accepted the collection fulsomely, and the book was reviewed respectfully everywhere when it came out.

# *HIGHWAYS TO A WAR*

The drawbacks of the house in Bilgola were such that Chris did not stay in it for much longer than two years before selling it for less than he had paid for it. Instead, imagining that he was moving to a climate similar to that of Tasmania, he bought a house in Leura, in the Blue Mountains. It was a comfortable two-storey house with space on the upper floor for a book-lined, immaculately carpentered study. Piers Laverty named the house "The Eagle's Nest", as he had taken to calling Chris "The Fuhrer" in an ironic reference to Koch's supposed right-wing political views. By this time, I had met Dick Connolly's niece, Margaret, who was working as an agent at Curtis Brown, and soon Chris had transferred his representation from Tim Curnow (who was annoyed, even though he worked for the same company) to Margaret. Piers and Les drove up to Leura for lunches and dinners at this time, as did Margaret and I, but after less than a year in the cool mountain air Adrienne went out for a walk on her own in August with heavy snow on the ground, and was run over by a car that slipped on the icy road surface. Adrienne survived the accident, but when Chris visited her in the Mater hospital in Sydney, accompanied by Robert Gray and me, it was apparent that his feelings toward her had changed. Though they continued to live together for another year, Adrienne eventually moved out, and Chris was left on his own in Leura. In the meantime, Margaret and I had been married, and Chris attended the wedding along with Les (who gave a brilliant speech) and Piers (who appointed himself the wedding photographer); in the following year Chris also attended the baptism of our daughter Frances, but by then he was sometimes accompanied by Cynthia Blanche when we met for dinner, and Cynthia was present at his sixtieth birthday party at Carl Robinson's Vietnamese restaurant, the Old Saigon.

Carl Robinson was an American who had worked as a journalist in Vietnam and Cambodia in the 1970s; he had then married a Vietnamese woman, retired from journalism and moved to Sydney where he and his wife, Kim, started the restaurant. Chris was spending time with Carl in order to research the new novel he was working on, an idea that had come to him when he was invited to produce the script for a television documentary based on Tim Bowden's book *One Crowded Hour*, a biography of the war photographer Neil Davis who had been at school in Hobart with both Bowden and Koch. The documentary project fell through, but Chris was left with a mass of research material that he knew he could put to use. In the same month as the birthday party, Les and Piers drove up to Leura to have lunch with Chris in a restaurant that advertised a "Christmas in July" special. According to Chris, Les and Piers were dissatisfied with the cooking and the service, and decided to flee without paying for their meal, by way of the back entrance, but the waiter caught them in the passage beside the kitchen. Chris was ashamed of the pair of them and swore that he would have nothing more to do with either of them (Piers has a different version of the story to tell, but that is another matter). He sold the house in Leura, and moved back to Tasmania, finding a house in Launceston just a street away from where his first wife Irene lived.

Soon after the move, Margaret and I, along with our one-year-old daughter, flew to Launceston to stay for a week in September with Chris in his new house. As with each of the houses I had visited him in so far, the upstairs study was immaculate and highly organised. Until this week, we had not realised that Chris had a phobia of small children, which may explain both the break-up of his first marriage and the fact that Gareth was an only child. Frances was well-behaved in his house, but Chris was in constant terror that she might break, drop, or scribble on one of his neatly arranged possessions. All the same, Chris acted as our tour guide while we were there, showing us the sights of Launceston and even taking us up to the snowfields of Ben Lomond. He also showed us the manuscript of the ambitious novel he was at work on, provisionally titled "Van Diemen's Land".

At this stage, the projected work was to be a single novel, in four parts alternating between a contemporary narrative set in Tasmania, Cambodia and Vietnam, and a historic section set in the late 1840s. Chris had completed the first two sections (as he saw it) and gave them to me to read. The first section, narrated by a Launceston lawyer called Ray Barton who had been a childhood friend of Mike Langford, built to a climax when Ray, after Mike's presumed death, opened one of "the two calfskin-covered notebooks" in a locked room on the Langford family farm, to read the first few sentences: *"Aboard the hulk 'Medway'. They are talking about me, through the wall..."* The second section opened with: "They are talking about me, through the wall", so that it was easy to see how the alternating sections would be intertwined. Chris hoped that the alternating structure would not be too cumbersome, while admitting that he had so much research material to work with that he did not know how he would fit it into the space. In due course he took the decision to publish each section as a separate novel, but he continued to think of the two books as a single work—a "diptych", as he now began to call it—which he gave the title *Beware of the Past,* though he focused on completing *Highways to a War* before returning to the second section.

The main reason he had given for showing me the work in progress was his concern about the use of punctuation in the projected novel: he had decided to leave the transcripts of Mike Langdon's tapes more or less unpunctuated, without quote marks and with each paragraph introduced by a dash. This, he hoped, would give the twentieth century section of the novel a feeling of informality suited to Langdon's character; but he had not yet made up his mind as to what to do about the punctuation in the nineteenth century section. Would it seem plausible for Robert Devereux, in his private journal, to make similar use of the dash? I offered an opinion, but in the end the decision was his, and the absence of quote marks means that the fictional journal has a contemporary freshness that a painstaking recreation of nineteenth century prose would lack.

Only two months after our visit to Launceston, Margaret resigned from Curtis Brown to establish her own literary agency, based in our house in Paddington; Chris, like all of her other Curtis Brown clients, eventually left with her. When the time came for *Highways to a War* to be placed with a publisher, Margaret settled on William Heinemann Australia, who would also publish the book in the United Kingdom just as Heinemann had first published *Across the Sea Wall*, and whose Managing Director then was my brother Sandy. Chris was anxious for his work to be published internationally, as it had been from the beginning of his career, so he sent the manuscript of *Highways to a War* to the notorious New York agent Andrew Wylie, known as "The Jackal", who responded positively at once. Chris delighted in imitating Wylie's deep, rich voice coming on the phone and greeting him with "Christopher." Wylie sold the book for a hundred thousand American dollars (a very large sum at that time) to Penguin, who then made no great effort to promote it, while Wylie disappeared.

It was in Australia that *Highways to a War* was most successful, earning Chris his second Miles Franklin Award. But by this stage he had a new imagined enemy, the freelance critic and editor of *Scripsi* magazine, Peter Craven, who wrote a weekly column for *The Australian*'s Higher Education page, and who had alluded to Koch as an author of "airport fiction". At the presentation ceremony for the Miles Franklin Chris gave a speech that was well-written and logically explained, deploring the state of literary teaching in the universities where "scholars released the plague called deconstructionism", and pointing out that "behind it stands the shadow of totalitarianism". Thirty years later, that speech appears perfectly reasonable, but it was briefly controversial among a few academics and journalists. Yet for Chris there was a greater source of alarm: as he gave the speech he noticed Peter Craven in the audience, glaring at him across the room.

*Highways to a War* is very far from being a work of "airport fiction", though it soon develops the narrative drive that would propel a thriller. It begins with the chapter I had read in Launceston, itself set in Launceston and then on the Derwent Valley hop farm near New Norfolk where Ray Barton and Mike Langford had spent teenage holidays. The Tasmanian landscape is evoked as vividly in these opening scenes as it is in *The Boys in the Island* (in an Author's Note to one of the reprinted editions of that novel it is revealed that the fictional village of Greendale where Heather Miles lives is "a rough composite of the towns of New Norfolk and Richmond") or *The Doubleman*, as Ray Barton returns to the farm and finds "Here were the upright golden flames of the poplars lining the road, and the willows yellowing down by the creek. Here were the hop fields, and elms and pines and cedars: the country of early settlement, rich and Europeanised... In the field on the other side of the road, the stripped wires and poles, bare of hops, were like ruined structures in a war zone", and at once the description puts the landscape's beauty before the reader's eye, and hints by way of the choice of metaphors at the flames and ruined structures that are to come.

As a boy, "Mike read a great deal", and his reading has something in common with that of Francis Cullen, who becomes fascinated by the "little racing pictures of a life locked beyond him, like the adventures of Felix the Cat", and the comic strips read by Richard Miller in his illness, and the childhood reading of Hugh Dixon in *Lost Voices*, *Felix the Cat* and *Terry and the Pirates*: to Mike, what is "more interesting to us" than any book is "a collection of weekly coloured supplements" that "featured serialised comic strips." "One strip fascinated Mike more than any other, to the point of obsession: Milton Caniff's *Terry and the Pirates*", and this obsession, like the metaphor describing the hop fields, anticipates Mike's future, in the comic strip's "beautiful villainess" called "The Dragon Lady". For Koch, one of the central preoccupations in his work entailed exploring the influence of childhood interests—interests, that is, rather than experiences—on adult behaviour. This is the reverse of the Freudian insight that character is formed by childhood trauma. The particular comic strips that recur through several of his novels are there, however, not just because the young Koch himself, as a future cartoonist and illustrator, found them interesting, but because in his opinion they were equally present in the childhood of an entire generation (this opinion might have been justified, if it needed to be, by the fact that the two newcomers to Australia's Test cricket team in 1961, Bill Lawry and Graham McKenzie, were given nicknames derived from comic strips by their team-mates).

In Saigon, the Dragon Lady, for Mike, is Madame Phan, but before he leaves New Norfolk he becomes involved in an affair that both echoes Brian Brady's lost love for Hazel Pearce in *The Doubleman* and foreshadows (or echoes) Robert Devereux's passion for Kathleen O'Rahilly in *Out of Ireland*, with Maureen Maguire, one of the hop-pickers on the family farm, "a red-haired girl" with "prominent cheek-bones" and blue eyes which were "wide-set and somewhat slanting." Maureen's rape and subsequent disappearance prompt Mike to leave the farm, and Tasmania, to embark on his career as a cameraman—the rapist, a sinister hermit called Luke Goddard, bears a certain resemblance, in his actions and his appearance, to the equally sinister Long Lane in *Out of Ireland*. Langford's occupation, of course, is the same as that of Billy Kwan in *The Year of Living Dangerously*, and he even uses the same film camera, a Bell and Howell, at the outset. At first one might suppose that the sole purpose behind the beautifully written scenes set in New Norfolk is to form a link between the two sides of the diptych, but Mike's attachment to Maureen is the first sign of his attachment to lost causes, and also of his compassion for vulnerable females like the crippled Kim Anh. Claudine Phan is not so vulnerable—"Maybe I'm a bit of a witch", she says—but she brings the part of the Dragon Lady from those childhood comic books to life; when Mike makes his first visit to her, "riding in a cyclo", the cyclo boy who pedals him to the address murmurs into his ear, "Everybody know Madame Phan... She is dragon lady."

The lost cause supported both by Madame Phan and by Mike Langford is that of the South Vietnamese Army, the ARVN. By joining the ARVN on patrols, Mike obtains film footage and still photographs that "set him on his way internationally", but he also takes risks that endanger his life. The imagery and incidental detail in these action scenes from the Vietnam War have not been surpassed by any Australian writer (it is interesting to compare them with the scenes on the Western Front in Martin Boyd's

*Where Blackbirds Sing*), and as is usual in a Koch novel they cause the pace of the narrative to accelerate; Harvey Drummond, one of the witnesses to Mike Langford's story, is speaking: "Pebbles and pink dust and emerald leaves were all in bits, in disconnected fragments, bright and precise, flying by me. I'd lost the Soldiers Three, and badly wanted to find them. Helicopter gunships had now appeared over the trees, insidiously throbbing, searching like intelligent insects". Soon after this, Langford is struck in the head by shrapnel, and as he lies on the ground with his face "covered by a shining red screen of blood that oozed and moved" his lips move: "'Somebody find my lucky hat,' he said."

The Soldiers Three are Mike Langford and his fellow-cameramen, Jim Feng and Dmitri Volkov. They have been given that nickname by the company of journalists and others who gather in a bar not unlike the Wayang Bar in *The Year of Living Dangerously*, but there are fewer scenes set in the bar and more in the battle zone than in the earlier novel. "Most combat cameramen, undergoing the risks they do together, regard one another as brothers", and it is that brotherhood that leads to the most powerful section of *Highways to a War*, where Langford, Feng and Volkov, at Mike's urging, go to Kompong Cham in Cambodia at a time when it "just wasn't a place to be". "Kompong Cham, fifty miles to the northeast, was an important city: a crossroads on the Mekong, strategically vital. But nearly all of Kompong Cham Province had now fallen to the North Vietnamese and the Khmer Rouge, and the rest was going fast. The city itself was said to be about to fall." Transported by a taxi driver in a "battered green Peugeot", they go to film two Government battalions in a "firefight" with the Khmer Rouge only for the taxi driver to be killed in an ambush while the "remnants of the battalion" escaped down the road. When they set out to walk to safety they are captured by "three soldiers in the uniform of the Army of North Vietnam".

What follows is a gripping weeks-long march along the Ho Chi Minh Trail while the three cameramen come to know, and almost to sympathise with, their captors. Once it is understood (after a terrifying interrogation) that they are neutral members of the press rather than American soldiers they are treated in a manner that is "courteous and considerate" by Captain Danh, the leader of the patrol that holds them captive. Five days into their march, the captives are allowed to join their guards as they eat from the "common pot" of rice that feeds them all, and Dmitri Volkov, whose aristocratic Russian heritage means that his family were victims of the Revolution, turning him into a fierce anti-communist, discusses Hegel with the captain. "I believe Hegel to be right, Danh said. We can only be truly moral and free if we subordinate ourselves to the State. This is a paradox—but true." "Hegel gave us Marx, who used the same argument, Dmitri put in. And Marx gave us Stalin and Mao Tse-tung, and so people didn't gain freedom, but lost it. And millions were liquidated." By making this argument, Volkov has brought a death sentence on himself, one that is carried out just as it seems the three cameramen have reached safety; yet the debate between Volkov and the captain is the most powerful, and significant, section of the novel, as both sides of the argument are set out in detail, and with considerable elegance: "This is an elegant argument of the Hegel's, Captain, Dmitri was saying. I sympathise with your reasons for accepting it." Of the two characters involved in the debate, Captain Danh is the most sympathetic and humane, while Volkov is such a prickly and self-destructive figure that it is easy for a reader to miss the fact that his arguments are the ones the author believed in. While writing the novel, Koch hoped that readers would not be able to deduce from this debate his own true position.

The debate is anticipated earlier in the novel when Langford meets Aubrey Hardwick, the Australian Embassy official with "blond-white, brutally crew-cut hair" and "watchful" eyes, who may be a government spy, and who tells him, "You should study the French and Russian revolutions if you're to cover what's going on in this part of the world." On the Ho Chi Minh Trail one of the guards, given the nickname "Lenin" by his captives, who appears to be a "Communist Party cadre", one "whose job was to report on the leader", is a spy of the most threatening kind. The interesting thing about the business of espionage, even when it is portrayed in the work of commercial writers like Le Carré, is the light it beams on the workings of the political world, both now and in historical times—hence the emphasis on the French and Russian revolutions in *Highways to a War*; in the companion volume, *Out of Ireland*, the French revolution is still fresh in the minds of the characters who have been exiled to Van Diemen's Land in the wake of the ill-fated revolutions of 1848.

All of those revolutions, including the Russian one, arose out of the philosophy of "Romanticism". The Romantic poets of the early nineteenth century (Wordsworth said of the French revolution "Bliss was it in that dawn to be alive") are an expression of that pervasive philosophy, and the jailed Irish rebels in *Out of Ireland* are prone to quoting from Shelley and Coleridge. Mike Langford is a Romantic in the sense that we think of the expression today, with his attraction to lost causes like that of the South Vietnamese and then of the Khmer in Cambodia, and also in his romantic attachments to women from Maureen Maguire on the New Norfolk farm, to Diana Lockhart in Launceston, Kim Anh and Madame Phan in Saigon, and finally to Ly Keang, known jokingly by the other correspondents as "the Battambang Stringer", in Phnom Penh. Most of these women are lost causes as well, or they are literally lost, as Maureen, Kim Anh and Ly

Keang all disappear, while Diana is married to one of Mike's best friends. His search for the missing Ly Keang takes Mike over the Cambodian border after the Khmer Rouge have taken control of the country and leads to his seeming death by crucifixion. The religious implications of his death cannot be ignored, and yet it is presented with a certain ambiguity, as hearsay, so that the narrator, Ray Barton, and the reader cannot be certain of what has happened. With religion, as with politics, Koch was always careful to leave his personal convictions unclear and unstated on the page, yet it is the combination of highly thoughtful and well-informed political discussion with suggestions of the spiritual that make him a major novelist, and *Highways to a War* a major novel.

# *OUT OF IRELAND*

In his domestic arrangements, Chris Koch himself was for much of his life an habitual Romantic, as can be seen as much from his constant house-moving as from his changes of live-in companion. *Highways to a War* was completed while he lived in Launceston, but in the next few years he was a frequent visitor to Sydney, often staying with friends in Paddington such as John Clark, the head of NIDA, who Chris had known since they were in kindergarten in Hobart. Much as he liked Tasmania, Chris missed his Sydney friends, with the exception of Piers, who he had decided to avoid; he had reconciled with Geoff Lehmann after appearing on the government's Honours List with an AO, for which Geoff had nominated him (I was asked to provide a statement of support for the nomination). Then in March of the year after *Highways to a War* was published Chris turned up in Sydney as a newly-wed: he introduced me to his new wife, Robin, who he had met in Tasmania even though she was originally a country girl from the region in New South Wales where Les Murray still lived. Robin had been married and divorced previously, and was the adoptive mother of a South East Asian orphan. The Miles Franklin presentation took place three months after the wedding. A few months later, our house in Paddington was sold and Margaret and I prepared to move to the Upper North Shore suburb of Warrawee, my father's childhood locality, adjoining Wahroonga, where Piers Laverty lived. At about the same time, by his account, Chris Koch was listening to a talk-back radio show on the ABC, late at night in his study in Launceston, when one of the programme's callers was Piers Laverty; impelled by nostalgia, and reminded of the humour that had enhanced his dinner parties, Chris broke his vow never to speak to Piers again and dialled his number. Soon he learned that the Wahroonga house next door to Piers was up for sale, at a good price. Thus, Chris sold the Launceston house, and soon he and Robin were near neighbours of mine, as well as even nearer neighbours of Piers.

For the next two years, Chris was at work on *Out of Ireland,* and I often joined him for coffee in a Wahroonga cafe where the Lebanese owners came to see him as a mascot. At first he wanted to discuss the diction in the history-based second half of his diptych: his concern was that the language should not mimic the style of nineteenth century prose, as do some historical novelists, and yet he did not want to allow his fictional diarist, Robert Devereux, to use expressions that only came into common usage in more recent times. He hoped to achieve a neutral diction that could plausibly have been used in the earlier century without lapsing into anachronism. To this end he made use of the *Jail Journal* of John Mitchel, the real-life Irish rebel, one of the leaders of the Young Ireland rising, who was the model for Devereux, and who Koch saw as the first writer of a high literary standard to describe the Tasmanian landscape. The name Robert Devereux originally belonged to an ancestor of Koch, one who was not convicted of any crime; the only difference between Mitchel's and Devereux's experience at first is that the latter (the fictional Devereux, that is, not the Koch ancestor) is imprisoned on the hulk "Medway" in Bermuda Harbour, while Mitchel was on the neighbouring hulk "Dromedary" (Koch may have changed the name of the hulk to avoid confusion, later, with Mount Dromedary near Hobart). Like Devereux, Mitchel heard the gangs at their dinner-hour talking about him through the wooden walls of his cell: "B—— his b——— eyes! What is he but a convict, like the rest of us—a d———, b——— convict?" This is the actual speech of a nineteenth century convict; Devereux hears "through the wall" "—Bugger his eyes! What is he but a convict, like the rest of us? That's right! A buggering, bloody convict!" The near identity of these two passages might allow a hostile reader to suspect Koch of plagiarism, but in fact the context in which the subtly altered version of these sentences (with once unprintable words spelled out) is placed at the beginning of Devereux's journal is an example of the structural skill that is a feature of the novel. Mitchel's version appears half way through the published edition of his journals, which for all their fine qualities are rambling and digressive when compared with the fictional journal created by Koch.

Another instance of the use Koch made of Mitchel's writing comes when, in Bermuda, a convict servant comes into Mitchel's cabin with a pineapple sent by the assistant surgeon: "The man was about 50 years of age, but very stout and active-looking, and highly consequential in his manner, as it soon turned out he had a good right to be. 'I trust, sir.' said he, 'you will find everything as you wish here: if I can do anything for you, I'm sure I shall be happy—I'm Garrett.' 'Well, Garrett?' quoth I.' 'Garrett, sir, *Garrett*; you must know all about me; it was in all the papers; Garrett, you know.' 'Never heard of you before, Garrett.' 'Oh! dear, yes, sir, you must be quite well aware of it—the great railway affair, you remember.' 'No, I do not.' 'Oh! then I am Mr Garrett, who was *connected with* the ——— railway (I forget the name of the railway). It was a matter of 40,000 I realised. Forty thousand pounds, sir: left it behind me, sir, with Mrs Garrett: she is living in England in very handsome style.'" Mitchel, in other words, had met the nineteenth century's version of Ronald Biggs; but Koch took this encounter and expanded the character of Garrett, renaming him James Langford, to establish the essential link between the two halves of the diptych:

> —I expect you'll have heard of me, sir, he said.
> I looked up guardedly from my sausages and eggs.
> —Heard of you, Langford? No; Doctor Howard has told me nothing about you.
> —Not through Doctor Howard, sir. Through the newspapers.
> He waited with quiet confidence for this to penetrate; the disturbing eyes steady on my face, hands at his side in military fashion. But I shook my head.
> —No. Never heard of you, Langford. I'm sorry. He smiled tolerantly.
> —You're just not remembering, sir, I expect. The South Eastern Railway Gold Affair. It realised a matter of five thousand pounds. I'm *that* James Langford.
> He watched me now with the quiet certainty of a man who did not need to advertise himself. I put down my knife and fork and stared back; but without comprehension.
> —That's right, he said quietly. Five thousand pounds, and not one farthing of it recovered by the authorities. Surely you recall the case now, sir?

Far from providing incriminatory evidence to those who might suspect Koch of plagiarism, these excerpts exemplify the manner with which he went about adapting Mitchel's authentic historical documents to create a credible language for his fictional, yet factually based, characters. The real-life experiences of Mitchel and the imagined ones of Devereux are similar in outline, yet the points where those experiences differ are revelatory. To read *Jail Journal* and *Out of Ireland* side by side is to be present at a systematic demonstration of the art of a novelist who can transform real events into a compelling narrative. John Mitchel was sentenced to "fourteen years' transportation" for his part in the failed "revolution" of 1848 in Ireland, but the British Government delivered "instructions" that he was to be treated not as a "common convict" but as "a person of education and a gentleman". After ten months on the hulk in Bermuda he was removed to Van Diemen's Land where he was given a "ticket-of-leave" on the condition that he promise not to "escape from the colony". Robert Devereux, in *Out of Ireland*, follows the same course until his arrival in the colony, at which point their paths diverge. Mitchel was joined in Bothwell by his wife and family, whereas Devereux became a single man, open to the kind of romantic involvements that propel a novel, after his fiancée, Catherine Edgeworth, broke their engagement by letter while he was on board the "Medway". Mitchel's time in Van Diemen's Land was relatively uneventful, though he was able to make many observations of the landscape and colonial society, and after only a few years he was able to escape to America. Devereux, too, escapes to America, but his years in Van Diemen's Land are far more dramatic and compelling to read about. His story is a tragedy in reverse as he journeys from the depths of near suicidal despair, brought about by his own tragic flaws, to a pastoral and romantic redemption followed by a successful escape that allows the reader to imagine his life continuing beyond the bounds of the novel.

The key to his redemption is James Langford: unlike Garrett, who disappears from Mitchel's journal almost immediately, Langford is sent to Van Diemen's Land at the same time as Devereux, and their connection continues when Langford is encountered as a convict servant at Bay House, home of Doctor Neville Howard, the kindly, affable surgeon on Bermuda who had sent a pineapple to the gentleman prisoner on the hulk, and who has accepted an appointment in Van Diemen's Land as Colonial Surgeon. Gradually it dawns on Devereux that Doctor Howard had been sent by the British authorities to spy on him—as in *Highways to a War*, espionage is a recurring theme in this novel—but first he allows Howard, who is an amateur artist, to paint his portrait, and the result is the painting discovered by Ray Barton and Mike Langford in the locked room on the Langford farm a century later. In Howard's studio, Devereux notices another painting, a female nude, and realises that the subject is Kathleen O'Rahilly, another one of the convict servants at Bay House, the implication being that Howard is at the least a voyeur if not something worse. When Langford invites Devereux to become his partner in a hop farm at New Norfolk—Langford's way of laundering his ill-gotten fortune—Devereux sees this as a way for him to rescue the Irish housemaid with eyes "set wide apart, and of a light sky-blue" from Howard's unwanted attention.

While John Mitchel and his unusual position as a "gentleman" convict is the starting point for *Out of Ireland*, the entirely imaginary narrative that follows Devereux's arrival in Van Diemen's Land is based loosely (as loosely as Joyce's *Ulysses* is based on Homer) on Dante's *Inferno*, a book Devereux mentions among his reading on the island. The scenes on the hulk in Bermuda, the voyage across the world to the place of exile, and then the descending depravity through the slums of Hobart Town, culminating in Black Lion Square, echo Dante's descent through the circles of Hell, and the epigraphs chosen for the second and third sections of the novel come from Dante as well. While Devereux, like Mitchel, is able to escape, a number of his fellow-exiles are not so fortunate, including Martin Fitzgibbon (whose character is based, up to a point, on the Irish rebel William Smith O'Brien, who in fact was released at the end of his sentence), Liam Kinane, and

Kathleen O'Rahilly, who all come to tragic ends, so that Devereux writes in his journal "It's as though some force is moving to destroy us one by one." The structure, like the classical structure Joyce used to frame *Ulysses,* adds significance and universality to the incidents recounted in the narrative, and yet one need not even be aware of its existence to find the story compelling.

Beyond the Dante-based structure, though, a second layer of structure shapes the narrative of *Out of Ireland* in the form of the parallels with the narrative of *Highways to a War.* Apart from the blood connection between Devereux (the diarist fathers a son with Kathleen O'Rahilly, who dies soon after giving birth, and the child is raised by the Langfords after Devereux makes his escape) and his direct descendant Mike Langford, perhaps the most important parallel is with the revolutionary ideas of the Young Irish exiles (though they disagree among themselves about the details) and the implementation of those ideas more than a century later by the North Vietnamese and the Khmer Rouge in Cambodia. Thus, Devereux and Captain Nguyen Van Danh have much in common: both are convinced that a communist, nationalist revolution is a necessity for the liberation of their country, and both are attractive characters that the reader cannot fail to identify with. The arguments against their revolutionary ideals are put to them by less sympathetic characters who both have underlying flaws, in Doctor Howard and Dmitri Volkov. The extended dialogues between Devereux and Howard, at first in Bermuda and then in Van Diemen's Land, echo the discussions on the Ho Chi Minh Trail between Volkov and Captain Van Danh. The arguments for both sides are expressed with clarity and intellectual depth, allowing the reader to make a choice between them; subsequent events, both in the novels and in the greater world, may have shown which ideas are correct, but Koch himself is careful, on the page, not to reveal the side that he favours—he is like Doctor Howard, who tells Devereux "I sail under neutral colours."

Even though Devereux, as the narrator of his own story, is obviously the character that the reader must identify with, the fact is that he is a terrorist who has been transported to Van Diemen's Land for advocating "flames and blood" in order to "see my country gain its freedom". Though he insists repeatedly throughout his narrative, "I am not a violent man" he is forced in self- defence to shoot two Irish bushrangers after they have kidnapped Kathleen, so that his friend the elderly bookseller Jacob Lenoir teases him, "You are not a violent man: I see. You are feared by the authorities as a terrorist, and you have just shot and killed two men—but you are not a violent man." The episode with the bushrangers anticipates the plot of *Lost Voices*, and it even includes a fleeting reference to Martin Cash, the model for Liam Dalton in the later Koch novel. Yet it is the Frenchman Lenoir, who shelters Devereux after he has withdrawn his parole, or promise, to the authorities not to attempt an escape, who reminds the reader of the parallels with Dante and with the Celtic fairy tales that also haunt *The Doubleman.* Lenoir urges Devereux to "climb back to the world", explaining "I made the mistake I warn you against. I came here to the Antipodes—truly to the Underworld!—in order to die to the world. For fifteen years I have lived among shadows. Now it's too late to go back... But you in your youth and strength—no. No, Devereux, you must not do this. Go: catch your ship, sail out of the Underworld, and live!"

Although Devereux refers to the place as Dis, and as the Underworld, and finally in his letter to Thomas O'Neill from the safety of San Francisco as "Inferno's ninth and final circle", Koch cannot conceal his attachment to the beauty of Tasmania. Of all his novels, *Out of Ireland*, despite its title, is his most extended hymn to the landscape, the lakes and hills, the "double-humped mountain called Mount Direction", and the river "which gleamed silver and broad below". He describes a ride in a "gig",

> through long shadows cast by the trees, passing ordered orchards of apple, plum and cherry, where the blue-winged native parrots darted like creatures of fancy. There were shadow-barred nut-walks here, and neat green fields dotted with fat cattle, and gravelled driveways and lawns, and many-coloured beds of immigrant flowers, and handsome stone villas in the Regency manner.

Throughout the novel there are similarly lyrical passages that recall the long-standing impulse toward poetry in Koch that had its first expression in *The Boys in the Island,* a prose book that originated in poetry. To further express that impulse, Koch made his character Martin Fitzgibbon an aspiring, but not very good, poet who torments his fellow-exiles by reading his poems aloud at every opportunity: in Thomas O'Neill's cottage in Bothwell he reads a poem that is quoted in full, that Chris delighted in showing to me, in manuscript form, as proof of his ability to write bad verse when required. Devereux observes of the poem "I dread hearing his efforts, since he quite lacks genius."

For its poetry as much as for its range of ideas about politics, philosophy and religion; for the racing speed of its plot as much as for its characterisation and psychological insights into imagined personalities; and above all for the ambitious architecture that frames the story, *Out of Ireland* is in my opinion the most important of the eight Koch novels, encompassing the most complete expression of his understanding of human nature in all its facets and delivering an extended and detailed tribute to the places and scenes that he never ceased to think about. Chris himself felt it to be his most significant work, and he was eager for it find an international audience as his first novel had done. In his eagerness, he was unable to accept that the publishing industry, both in Australia and internationally, had changed since 1958. In the period just after the Second World War, it was easier for an Australian novelist to find a publisher in Britain than in the far-flung dominion where the book industry only existed to distribute works from overseas; by 1999 there was a considerable range of Australian imprints to choose from (though many of them were local outposts of British companies), while publishing in Britain and America was far more parochial than it had been when Koch made his debut. Wylie the jackal was no longer interested in representing Christopher, so instead he approached the English agent David Godwin who expressed polite enthusiasm, even coming to lunch in the garden at Wahroonga, but then did nothing. The enthusiasm of Australian publishers was much more genuine, and in the end Margaret negotiated a deal with Doubleday, an imprint by then of the Random House group that had in recent years swallowed most of the leading British publishers of former days, including the original publishers of *The Boys in the Island* and *The Doubleman*.

The Doubleday edition, for which I acted as copy-editor (though an in-house editor suggested that the novel be transformed into a feminist polemic, with stronger female characters and less chivalrous males, a suggestion indignantly rejected by Chris), was widely praised, and even won the Victorian Premier's Prize for Fiction, but there was one exception to its otherwise universal acclaim—a review by Peter Craven, who noted that *Out of Ireland's* action-packed plot and lucid prose style made the novel as readable as any best-seller, an observation that most novelists would have accepted as praise. For Chris, though, this was a "knife-job" from his enemy, intended as revenge for his speech at the Miles Franklin presentation. The only solution, he believed, would be for someone to write a letter to the editor of *The Australian*, where the review had appeared, and for that someone to be me. This did not seem like a good idea to me, so I wrote an eloquent letter addressed to the editor, and showed it to Chris, but then never posted the letter, having pointed out to him that not every letter to the editor achieves publication.

# *THE MEMORY ROOM*

When *The Boys in the Island* and *Across the Sea Wall* were reissued by Angus & Robertson in the late 1980s the junior editor responsible for seeing the reprint through the publishing process was a young woman called Nikki Christer. By the time *Out of Ireland* was attracting some public interest, Nikki Christer had ascended through the hellish circles of the book business to become the publisher of the Picador imprint at Pan Macmillan. Remembering her old acquaintance with Koch, she invited him to make a return to the Ireland of his ancestors, with the assistance of the Irish Tourist Board, and write a non-fiction book about his experiences. The result was *The Many-Coloured Land*, which is something more than a mere travelogue, as the account of his journey and his meetings with friends and distant relatives turns a light on the background to many of the obsessions and themes of his fiction, from the Celtic fairy tales and folk music of *The Doubleman* to the historic facts behind *Out of Ireland*. Though the book is a work of non-fiction, Chris took the work very seriously, and he became very concerned about the dangers of faulty proof-reading, so that he decided the only way to avoid typographical slip-ups was to use the proofreading method he remembered from his days at the Hobart *Mercury* in the 1950s, where one man read the words aloud while another checked the pages. Thus, it was that I came to spend several afternoons sitting in the elegantly furnished upstairs study in the house at Wahroonga while Chris read his book aloud as I pored over the page proofs.

Chris enjoyed these sessions so much that we would repeat the process for his next novel, *The Memory Room*. First, though, he had to write it, and there was an obstacle to his usual writing routine in the form of Piers, his next-door neighbour. Piers was the entrepreneurial owner of a tree-lopping business, and his team of climbers, stump-grinders and branch-draggers had taken to meeting at Piers's house early each day to warm up their chainsaws amid loud conversations while at the same time there were noisy building renovations in progress at the house, with drills and hammers echoing through the neighbourhood. The racket, first thing in the morning, was such that Chris went to Piers to protest about it, explaining "I'm trying to write a book." Piers replied, "You don't need to write a book. There's a shop in Wahroonga that'll sell you one." Les Murray found this response hilarious, and even wrote a poem about it:

> The man next door
> cursed our builders' noise.
> He was writing a book,
> so we scoffed, through the hedge,
> Shops would sell him a book!
>
> ("King Lear Had Alzheimer's")

The rift between Chris and Les, which had already widened since Les published his verse novel *Fredy Neptune*, became almost unbridgeable. Yet throughout the years that the two of them were estranged, I was in constant contact with both, sometimes on alternate days, so perhaps I could have been regarded as the bridge—each took the opportunity to vent his frustration and disapproval of the other while talking with me.

Chris felt that he needed to write a new novel

because he was increasingly anxious about his finances. While working on *The Many-Coloured Land* he had also agreed to write the script for a film version of *Highways to a War* to be produced by Bruce Beresford, who he met with several times. When the project fell through Chris told me that he worried he might end his days like the poet Roland Robinson, living on his own in a boat shed. He also told me that he felt like Dostoevsky, according to Chris an incurable gambler who would lose everything he owned, even his wife's wedding ring, at the tables, then return home to beg forgiveness on his knees, saying "Only the novel can save us."

The novel that Chris thought might save him did not take long to echo previous works: on its first page, we read "Out in the east, twin-humped Mount Direction has appeared, rising above the steep, orange-tiled roof". The main theme of the novel is familiar also, as the central character, Vincent Austin, finds himself "caused to mull over certain things that have a particular, private importance for me. Principal among these is my interest in espionage". At about this time Chris had been in regular contact with Warren Reed, a former ASIO operative, who was himself writing a novel that Chris persuaded Margaret to place with a publisher—Reed was the only visitor to our house who tried to leave by way of the linen cupboard rather than the front door, so that we had to doubt his capability as a real-life spy; he was certainly not the model for the meticulous Vincent Austin. Chris showed me the first fifty pages of *The Memory Room*, and only a few weeks later told me that he had decided to move back to Tasmania, having bought a house in Richmond, the historic village with its "Georgian villas, miniature stone cottages and aged stone bridge" that features in those early pages of the new novel as the location of the Austin family farm. Moving to Tasmania, it seemed, was the only way for him to escape the sonic bombardment of Piers and his chainsaws; the house that he had bought was not a "Georgian villa" but a relatively modern bungalow with a front room that looked over a panorama of the Coal River and the hills beyond, a room that was promptly converted into a study for Chris to work from.

"The upstairs verandah-sunroom at the front of the house" that Vincent Austin has converted into a study, with bookshelves and "the antique oak desk and office chair", immediately brings to mind the immaculate studies that Chris created for himself in each of his houses, while the physical description of the other leading character in *The Memory Room,* Derek Bradley, could well be a portrayal of Chris himself: "he was an 'easy' man. Now thirty-three, he looked younger, and would probably appear youthful well into middle age. His looks were pleasing, but had never been striking enough to arouse envy or irritation. Of medium height, he was athletically built, and remained as lean as he'd been in his twenties." "Twin-humped Mount Direction"—the view that strikes Bradley on the first page is the same one that Robert Devereux had seen more than a century earlier, and that "entranced" Richard Miller in *The Doubleman*; this is not mere repetition, but a reminder that the very different events in each of the novels take place against the same background. Thus, it is possible for one who reads all of them in sequence to imagine the different characters, in all their variety, existing together in that setting, and perhaps unknowingly passing one another in the street, at the same time, as apart from the historic period of *Out of Ireland* the years of the various narratives overlap.

My own first visit to Tasmania, in 1973, almost overlapped Vincent Austin's final year at the University of Tasmania, so I could not help pointing out to Chris that by 1972 the University's Political Science department was located in a soulless modern building at Sandy Bay rather than in the "stone, three-storey Gothic structure, built by our colonial founders in the nineteenth century, with buttresses and parapeted gables, covered with suitably ancient-looking ivy" in the centre of Hobart. Chris admitted that he had kept the old building for its literary effect, and he also admitted that by 1972 there were no longer trams running in Hobart—these two instances of fictional licence were rare exceptions to his usual attention to precise historic, and geographic, accuracy. The discussion arose while I was acting as editor of the completed manuscript. When page proofs of *The Memory Room* were available, I flew to Tasmania and stayed in the house at Richmond for several days while Chris and I performed our proof-reading double act; at the same time John Clark, the head of NIDA, was also a house-guest, and he and Chris bickered like the kindergarten pupils they had once been together.

*The Memory Room* is built around a structural device similar to most of the novels from *The Year of Living Dangerously* onward: a neutral observer, in this case Derek Bradley, Vincent Austin's friend from university days, has access to the diaries and papers of the absent central character: like Mike Langford, Vincent has disappeared, and it is possible to suppose that he has died, though his death is never referred to in the novel. Tasmanian readers of a certain age have been able to recognise in Vincent's story the case of an islander whose body was found at the base of a cliff near Hobart, who turned out to have connections with the secret service. Somewhat less than half of the narrative is drawn from Vincent's papers, while the rest is seen through the eyes of Bradley; the other central character is Erika Lange, a friend since childhood of Vincent Austin with a personality as devious and convoluted as that of Vincent. While writing the novel, Chris told me that he had based the appearance, and some of the actions, of Erika Lange on a friend of mine, a glamorous-looking lesbian who preferred to socialise with men, treating the women in her life as mere sex objects.

As with *Highways to a War*, the novel begins after the disappearance of its central figure, as Bradley enters the upstairs space in the house of Vincent's aunt Connie, who had raised her nephew since he was orphaned at the age of twelve, a room that had been dismissed as a mere "storeroom" when they sat beside its closed door in "wicker chairs" as undergraduates. He and Vincent (who likes to call him "Brad") both joined the Department of Foreign Affairs after graduating, but unknown to Bradley his friend with an appetite for secrecy had been recruited to ASIS, the Australian spy agency, by Ted Bobrowski, the professor of Political Science at the university where both of them studied. The conversations with Bobrowski recorded in Vincent's diary, found in the secret room, echo the discussions held by Mike Langford with Aubrey Hardwick, and by Dmitri Volkov with Captain Danh, and by Robert Devereux with Neville Howard, though in each case the questions of idealism, communism, religion, revolution and romanticism are approached from a different angle. Bobrowski, whose appearance "reminds one irresistibly of one of those cavern-dwelling dwarfs in European legend" responds to Vincent's remark "I've heard that Catholics make the best Communists" by saying "Although I am a Catholic, I acknowledge this. The virtues of Catholicism—devotion to dogma, conscious submission to an entire spiritual and intellectual system—are turned upside down in such cases, and made into a force for evil. As in witchcraft." Bobrowski is Polish, so he has had first-hand experience of the Soviet Empire's "intellectual system", from which he "had the good fortune to escape". In a hostile and inaccurate "knife-job" (as Koch called it), a reviewer in, of all places, the *Times Literary Supplement* described this eloquent and closely reasoned passage as an "anti-Marxist diatribe", something it very clearly is not.

Vincent's diary also records the strange connection he has with Erika Lange, the motherless daughter of a German immigrant, who becomes his childhood friend, sharing an interest (like Mike Langford) in the comic strips *Terry and the Pirates* and *Flash Gordon*, but who never forms a physical attachment to him ("You can look, but don't touch," she says, after getting Vincent to photograph her in the nude). When Vincent, Derek Bradley and Erika are all assigned to the Australian Embassy in Peking (the novel uses the old style of transcription for Chinese names) the strangeness of their association becomes apparent to Bradley when Erika starts an affair with him. For Bradley, Erika soon becomes an "addiction", one which "had shaken Bradley's usual equanimity." Erika is one of the strongest, most haunting female characters in all the novels Koch wrote, in part because the reader is familiar with her childhood by way of Vincent's diaries, and in part because even though both we and Bradley come to know more "in the factual sense" about Erika's life, "Somehow, nothing seemed certain about her."

Nothing is certain about Peking, either, with Communist Party cadres, spies and suspicious Government officials on every corner, yet Koch is able to evoke the beauty of the surviving culture and architecture, and of the surrounding landscape, the lakes, mountains and arched bridges, as well as the squalid tenements inhabited by those who do not belong to the ruling elite, with his accustomed attention to detail. For those details, he was helped by a journey he took through China many years before with Nicholas Hasluck, supported by the Literature Board.

Bradley's affair with Erika is brought to an end when he proposes marriage to her only to be told "I'm not ready", and the Peking sojourn for all three main characters comes to an abrupt conclusion when Vincent's scheme to arrange the defection of a distinguished Chinese scholar of literature to Australia is exposed by "their Ministry of State Security". Instead, both Bradley and Vincent are transferred to Canberra, where Koch, whose poetry-rich evocations of the cities of Hobart, Melbourne, Sydney, Jakarta, Madras, Delhi and Peking have already been an important feature of his novelist's achievement, adds another beautifully realised topographical account of an urban setting to his extensive repertoire of places. No other writer has captured the atmosphere of Canberra better, the "unnaturally flawless and orderly" creation that "functioned as a vortex of the nation's power", and yet "consisted of a set of model villages, each with its own shopping centre, occurring like islands among extensive bush reserves, and linked by curving, perfectly maintained highways."

In the capital, Vincent has been appointed to a position ("Let's call it Operational Co-ordinator") in the Registry of the new ASIS Main Office, recently moved from Melbourne, where the Director General explains to him "The Registry is our memory room—and you'll be the guardian of our memories." It is a job ideally suited to his orderly, classifying temperament, yet he remains in disgrace with his superiors for his ill-advised scheme in Peking. For an extended period, Vincent refuses to speak to Bradley after explaining "I see no immediate need to meet", his reason being that "I understand that you blame me in the matter of Professor Liu." After a year has passed Vincent allows contact to be resumed, and when Bradley, who has never blamed Vincent for his disgrace, asks "Who on earth says that I did?" The answer comes after "Vincent looked into his whisky. 'Erika,' he said. 'She wrote to me.' Bradley sat back. 'She was lying,' he said. 'Was she? That's possible,' Vincent said." This response, for me, recalls Margaret's favourite Chris Koch anecdote, about a meal he was served in a Spanish restaurant where he complained to the waiter that it seemed the fish on his plate was off. Stone-faced and deep-voiced, the waiter just replied, "Is possible." Vincent justifies Erika's duplicity by saying that she was "Emotionally shattered at the way you deserted her", even though Bradley understood that Erika had deserted him. Paradoxically, Erika, whose career as a journalist derives as much from her open and friendly manner as from her attractive appearance, is as devious as a spy, while Vincent, the professional secret agent, is honest and idealistic to his own disadvantage.

Erika, who becomes a successful television presenter with the help of secret information supplied to her from Vincent's Memory Room, is not the first character in a Koch novel to achieve prominence in the mass media. O'Brien, in *Across the Sea Wall*, becomes a journalist; Guy Hamilton, helped by Billy's Kwan's filming, gains a degree of celebrity for his reports from Jakarta in *The Year of Living Dangerously*, and Mike Langford in *Highways to a War* is equally celebrated for his television reports; the Rymers, in *The Doubleman*, are elevated to fame by the television show created by Richard Miller; and before the advent of television, Robert Devereux in *Out of Ireland* is a national celebrity on the strength of his journalism. In most of these cases, fame leads to a downfall, though Erika's downfall also results from her taste for secrecy that ends either with her suicide or murder—the actual reason for her death is left ambiguous. Her attachment to Peter Rykov, a Russian journalist who also happens to be "an officer of KGB, with the rank of major", is certainly a contributing factor, but Vincent's superiors will not allow him to investigate the matter further, hence his disappearance.

Rykov, whose speech patterns, often omitting the definite article, resemble those of Dmitri Volkov in *Highways to a War*, first befriends Vincent perhaps as a means of getting close to Erika; but it does not occur to Vincent to suspect this, noting in his diary that "I liked him, and his ebullience was infectious; but he was hard to read. He might well be what he seemed: a mercurial, easygoing journalist who was not over-respectful of the Soviet leadership." Rykov, after a shared drive from Sydney to Canberra, concludes that Vincent is "a crazy man… and probably a religious nut" after a discussion about Karl Marx in which Vincent proposes that Marx "denied the spirit. He hated God; he was at war with God." This is hardly an "anti-Marxist diatribe" on the part of the author, as Rykov is immediately "incredulous", and asks "Excuse me, but what is your evidence for this?" Vincent's justification for his assertion is a poem written by Marx that includes the line "*I wish to avenge myself against the One who rules above*", but Rykov in response "gave his big, full-throated laugh." Throughout the novel, as is the case through all of his novels, Koch returns to religion and the spiritual as a theme, even though Vincent insists that he is not religious, or at least "not in a conventional way". The numinous lies behind Vincent's conversation with Ted Bobrowski, and beneath Erika's dabbling with Tarot cards, and in this way it is raised in this discussion with Peter Rykov.

It is the spiritual dimension, in this novel as well as in all those that come before it, that suggests Koch must be considered as a major novelist. By way of contrast, few of those Australian novelists who might be his equal deal with religious matters in any fashion other than the negative. As with his political views, Koch is careful never to commit his private position to paper (he was raised as a Catholic, but for much of his life could have been described as "lapsed"), or to draw any conclusions, as spirituality is by its nature inconclusive. Instead he allows his characters to express a diversity of beliefs. For Vincent, who was influenced in childhood by his uncle Kenneth, a Presbyterian minister, a belief in the other world of the spirit turns into a longing to create another world of secrecy, and the central purpose of the novel is to explore the motivations of a professional spy, or Erika, who has a devious personality without formally engaging in espionage. Thus, even though its theme is espionage, *The Memory Room* is not a spy novel or a thriller: it is an intense examination of a specific psychological tendency.

As with each of the novels he had published since *The Year of Living Dangerously*, Koch won a major literary prize for *The Memory Room*. The circumstances of this award were unusual, in that I was a member of the judging panel that chose the book for the CAL Waverley Library Award for Literature. As I had acted both as editor and proofreader for the novel, it was necessary for me to keep silent when *The Memory Room* came up for discussion, but my fellow-judges, Ursula Dubosarsky and Kathleen Stewart, both chose the book as our prizewinner, and it was not my place to disagree with them. Chris travelled from Tasmania to Bondi Beach to accept the prize money, which he used to buy himself a second-hand car.

# *LOST VOICES*

For some time, Margaret had been trying to persuade Christopher to produce another work of non-fiction, perhaps along the lines of *The Many-Coloured Land*, if only to capture in print the wonderfully entertaining anecdotes he had recounted to her about his early years. Now, without an idea for a new novel, he started to write about his childhood in Hobart, about his days working in Fuller's Bookshop, and time as a cartoonist at the *Mercury*. The work stimulated his novelist's instincts, and before long what might have been a memoir was transformed into an ambitious novel. At the same time Chris had become dissatisfied with his publisher, Random House (owner of both the Doubleday and Knopf imprints), where Nikki Christer now worked, and their plan to make his back-list books available only as "print on demand" titles. The solution, for Margaret, was to sell the new novel to HarperCollins, where the former publisher at Doubleday, Shona Martyn was now in charge, as HarperCollins were also prepared to reprint the back-list titles. As before, I acted as editor and then proofreader of *Lost Voices*, and while I was working on the novel with Christopher, sitting in a leather armchair in his study with its sweeping view over the Coal River, he began to complain from time to time about pain in his back. When the novel was completed, and about to be published, the back pain had been diagnosed as lymphoma, and Christopher was too unwell to attend his own book launch, a lavish event held in the Henry Jones Art Hotel in Hobart, so that I was asked to appear in his place and deliver the following speech, which will suffice as a comment on this novel:

As you can see, I am not Christopher Koch. I am here as his delegate, while he recovers from illness. Yet I am able to do something he would be too modest to do himself, and that is to set out the reasons for all of us to see him not just as another award-winning literary novelist, nor as an author of best-sellers, though he is both of those things, but as Australia's finest living writer of fiction.

This is not the first time I have made this suggestion regarding his stature; it is one I believe it would have been possible to support even while Patrick White was still alive, and my purpose here is to touch on a few of the elements in Koch's writing which have led me, over the years, to reach that conclusion.

Chris Koch is not our only living novelist, and at different times we have all been subject to claims on behalf of the likes of David Malouf, Peter Carey, Tim Winton, Kate Grenville, Geraldine Brooks, Gerald Murnane, Murray Bail, Helen Garner, Thomas Keneally, Richard Flanagan, Christos Tsiolkas, and others too many to mention. This is not the time to be negative, but I will say that it is possible to demonstrate the superiority of Koch to each of these acclaimed authors by the old-fashioned method of close attention to the text.

If we pay close attention to the words on the page in the books of all the authors I have just listed, it soon becomes apparent that Koch exists on a different dimension. The qualities in his work can be measured on a scale, or a set of standards, we should all keep in mind while making imaginary hierarchies of literary merit. These standards, for a novelist, include such elements as plot, structure, characterisation, depth of content, and, perhaps most importantly, prose style.

When we open the pages of *Lost Voices* we find

each of these elements refined and polished to the highest degree. The plot is both intricate and perfectly balanced; it fulfils the memorable aphorism we find in the novel's first sentence, to the effect that "everything in our lives is part of a pre-ordained pattern". It is a plot that would serve just as well in a commercial, page-turning thriller—yet this is a plot in a novel with serious literary ambition. Incidentally, one of the more notable features of Koch as a novelist has always been his ability to produce a memorable opening sentence. Who can forget the way *The Year of Living Dangerously* begins: "There is no way, unless you have unusual self-control, of disguising the expression on your face when you first meet a dwarf"? In turn, he has also had such a memorable way with book titles that at least two of his have become cliches of the newspaper headline profession.

The structure of *Lost Voices* realises perfectly the scheme Koch thought of first in the early stages of what was to become the two separate yet interlocking novels *Highways to a War* and *Out of Ireland*. Originally, he thought of these two as a single novel, divided into four sections alternating between the twentieth and nineteenth centuries, but in the end the length of each segment grew to the point where it seemed less unwieldy to turn that single novel into a diptych.

The overall title of the diptych, *Beware of the Past*, could be applied to *Lost Voices* as well. In *Lost Voices*, we are presented with a novel within a novel, the twentieth-century memoir of Hugh Dixon's youthful dealings with his great-uncle Walter enclosing the story of Walter's father Martin and the events he was never able to forget. The two stories, this time, are seamlessly contained within a single volume, and characters from the nineteenth-century segment echo across the years with their twentieth-century counterparts, though these echoes are not schematic or heavy-handed.

Because Koch creates these structures with a light touch, the characters in all his novels come to life in such a way that one feels it would be possible to recognise them in the street. Indeed, Christopher and I walked into a Sydney coffee shop many years ago when a man at one of the tables invited us to join him: I knew at once, without being told, that this man was the model for Darcy Burr in *The Doubleman*, which had just been published. Christopher confirmed my thought as soon as the man had left. Frances Lambert and Moira Doran echo one another across the century-long span of *Lost Voices*, each of them embodying one of the skills for which Koch does not always receive due acknowledgement, which is the portrayal of strong female characters.

Similarly, Roy Griffin and Max Fell are linked as characters, as each embodies what Koch sees as a rarity, a being of pure evil, while Lucas Wilson and Walter Dixon are both kindly mentors to the younger Dixon men, both of them well-meaning yet flawed.

It is the content of all of Koch's novels that makes them something more than just an exciting adventure story, though each from *The Year of Living Dangerously* on can be read as such.

Beneath the clever plots, and the carefully worked-out structures, his novels deal with ideas essential to an understanding of society today, and of the essence of human nature. Through the views of Lucas Wilson, he is able to outline many of the political theories which took hold in the nineteenth century and were to have such an effect in the next century: Wilson is an idealist, who sincerely believes that he can create a perfect society run for the benefit of all who belong to it, yet his ideals can only be achieved by violence and the threat of violence. The existence of evil in the world, Koch shows us, has always been an insurmountable obstacle for political ideologies. Koch shows us these ideas, he does not tell us, for he is never didactic. Ideas in his novels emerge naturally from the mouths of his characters, as he is a master of believable dialogue. His skill in this area, where many novelists lose their readers' suspension of disbelief either by exaggerating vernacular expressions, or by allowing modern phrases into historical speech, lies in the plainness of the language spoken by his characters; as far as possible they use expressions that might as well be used today as more than a hundred years ago.

This simplicity of expression is the reason for the success of his historical fiction; it makes a novel like *Out of Ireland* read as universal story-telling, not as an elaborately concocted pseudo-historic document. In turn, this is the result of the most important of Koch's attributes as a writer, which is the sheer beauty of his prose style. His literary career began, long ago, with poetry, and he has always maintained an affinity with poets, which is why the character Alan McLeod in *Lost Voices* bears a distinct resemblance to Les Murray—like a film director, Koch likes sometimes to give walk-on roles to his friends. Of all those highly-regarded novelists mentioned earlier, including Patrick White, none can match Koch, sentence by sentence, for elegance, clarity and rhythmic effect. For me to make such an assertion, however, is not enough: the evidence for my claim can be demonstrated most effectively by a simple exercise, which is to open one of Koch's novels at random and read the first sentence before one's eyes.

When I performed this exercise with *Lost Voices*, the following passage appeared before me:

> He pointed across the land that lay everywhere below them. The afternoon was sunny, with a faint breeze, and they were walking across one of the hills in the east, through an open area of grass and boulders. They seemed to walk close to the sky, and Martin was

> buoyed up by an illusion of limitless freedom. Below them on the western side of the hill stretched a green open pasture where the dairy herd grazed, enclosed by a post-and-rail fence. Beyond this, on the far side of the valley, the dense hills of bush rose above the roofs of the settlement, and beyond these again stretched those long blue ranges, hazed with sun, which seemed to belong in another dimension. It was to these that Wilson had pointed.
>
> I study them for hours, he said, and I ask myself what it is they hide. Not just unexplored country, surely. No—something more. The entrance to a sphere beyond our knowledge. The dimension of the divine, perhaps.

This is more than one sentence, of course. One sentence, in this novel, leads irresistibly to the one that follows it, even though there are no clever linguistic tricks or ingenious, unlikely images to attract the reader's attention. The style is unadorned and direct, presenting a picture in words that is as easy to grasp as a landscape painting; and yet the writing is full of subtle echoes (fence/dense), alliteration (land/lay, buoyed/beyond/below/bush/blue) and repetitions (dimension/dimension) and half-rhymes (breeze/east) as a poem might be.

The implication that the writing in *Lost Voices* approaches the condition of poetry may seem off-putting to those in the audience who happen to be booksellers or publishers; poetry after all, has an unfortunate reputation for lack of commercial appeal. They should not, all the same, be put off for long. This extraordinary novel provides full value to paying customers: not only does it consist of two novels for the price of one, it really includes several types of book at once, all of them gathered together in a neat package. They include a childhood reminiscence, a study of art history, a book about first love, a gripping historical thriller, a murder mystery and a courtroom drama. Above all else, however, *Lost Voices* is a hymn of praise for Tasmania, and that is why we are all here in Hobart today.

***

In the years leading up to the publication of his final novel, Christopher had discovered a new imagined enemy to focus all his fears and furies upon: this was the Tasmanian novelist Richard Flanagan, whose writing seemed to be moving into the literary space that Koch had occupied, and who inflamed the situation further by telling an interviewer that he had heard of Koch but had never read him. In the Henry Jones Art Hotel, as I began to read out the text of my prepared speech, I was disconcerted to notice that Richard Flanagan (who had not been invited) had appeared at the back of the room. Thus, I repeated to myself, as I read, "Don't mention Flanagan", but when I came to the list of names in the speech quoted above where I should have said "Thomas Keneally" what came out through my mouth was "Thomas… Flanagan". There were those in the audience who suspected I had said it on purpose, but this was not the case.

The hope that my speech held out for his recovery was ill-founded, as cancer's deadly work was completed precisely a year and a day after the book launch; first, though, my speech was published in *Quadrant* magazine, where Les Murray continued to serve as Literary Editor. After all their years of estrangement, Chris was moved to send Les the following letter:

Dear Les,

It was good to get your *100 Best Poems* and the *Quadrant* anthology—and better still to hear that you liked *Lost Voices*. Since Jamie leaked the fact that the bushranger Alan McLeod owes some characteristics to you, I was a little nervous that you might take exception—though I hoped not, since he's a sympathetic character, as well as being a bard and a composer of songs. And as you well know from the past, I do no exact portraits, but simply borrow a few characteristics. I did the same with Lucas Wilson: I wonder if you glimpsed our long-gone bard Roland Robinson?

I'm glad that we're back in touch, and hope we'll remain so, if only at long distance. I had been thinking of writing to you for some time, and this resolve was made firmer by a recent and life-changing experience.

Over three months ago, after a lifetime of lucky good health, I was diagnosed with lymphoma, an aggressive cancer that attacks the bone, and was given three weeks or so to live. Then a remarkable specialist was called in who said she'd give me a chance of survival if I'd undergo a very tough form of chemotherapy which will only end this month. In seven weeks, the cancer has entirely disappeared. My GP (an agnostic) calls it a miracle, since he's never heard of anyone recovering that fast. As for me, I know it was a miracle, since I did some serious praying. God's granted me a little more time.

They say that surviving cancer changes you. I wouldn't say that it's changed me; what it has done is to make me value the visible world even more, and value my friends. My life has been uneven, but I'm glad of all the good memories, and you figure in many of these.

Ours was an important friendship—certainly for me—and sits at the centre of our lives. The days of our youth in Sydney (the Challis Avenue salon; the drives to Canberra and elsewhere) come back in a sunny glow.

Different in many ways, we were, I believe, always allies and like-minded in what matters most: truth and falsity in literature. On this we always agreed; and, yes, we are often laughing, in that past. As well, I'll always be grateful for the part you played in launching *The Year,* the book that changed my life, when you took it to B. Davis at Nelson.

I mention these things because at 80, I'm further down the road than you, and (as they say in America) I'll probably beat you to the barn. Let's hope for some more good years for both of us, but this is a good time to remain in contact.

Chris

# *EPILOGUE*

## *A WALK IN THE COAL RIVER VALLEY WITH CHRISTOPHER KOCH*

Two figures move along a deserted road
at the centre of a landscape of farms
and forest-capped slopes. A single car passes,
its driver raising one finger off the wheel
in the traditional countryman's
salute. The dust on the road is as real
as the images brought into someone's
mind, of the estuary and its arms
wrapped around townships and sheep-grazed grasses,
        waters that have flowed

down from mountainsides, long extinct cones
of ancient volcanoes. Of the two
walkers, one is myself, while the other
is a man who wears a cap one might see
on a Greek fisherman, a man with shrewd
eyes and a subtle grin, the delicacy
of an old watchmaker somehow imbued
in his manner, even if that is not who
he happens to be. Over the fields a plover
        tips its wings and moans

like a distant child. The thorny hedges
beside the road flourish scarlet berries
the size of tear drops; over the hillside
rows of grapevines are covered in plastic
nets, that flutter in the breeze like flags. Sheep
move slowly in a field, touching their thick
lips to the dust-pale earth. A stone house, deep
among shade-giving conifers; beady-eyed
swallows in the eaves, swooping in flurries
        like swarms of midges;

small birds among the vine-rows. Another house
beside the road, red brick with a tower
on one corner—and my companion tells
the history behind the tower's construction,
and talks about crop growth and old wealth.
His knowledge stretches over the fields, a distraction
from his thoughts about the declining health
which means he must suffer from hour to hour.
From far away, a sound of muffled bells;
            a scattering of cows

steeped in long grass; hills named after household
objects, sugarloaf, cap and bonnet, and
beyond those hills the unseen mountains, jagged
as Switzerland; lakes in hidden valleys,
like the waterways of Europe; small towns
laid out and built almost two centuries
before, beside creeks on flatlands and downs.
The earliest occupants of this land
left no buildings or sculptures, and wore rugged
            cloaks against the cold;

and yet while Napoleon was still alive,
while Lord Byron journeyed among the Greeks,
stone walls and bridges, churches and barracks
arose in forest clearings and on the banks
of rivulets—walls that remain standing
to this day. Buckets and water tanks
in cottage gardens; pathways winding
like the quiet voice of the one who speaks
to me now, of politics and income tax,
            the will to survive,

and the hazards of idealism. A hand
gestures as the words take shape in his thought
about the past and the present. This place
with its contours and its watercourses
has drawn him back whenever he has meant
to leave. A training track for racehorses
behind a modern farm house, shaped like a tent,
prompts a tale. All through his life he has sought
peace: this landscape written over his face,
          Van Diemen's Land.

www.ingramcontent.com/pod-product-compliance
Lightning Source LLC
Chambersburg PA
CBHW050012040726
47599CB00014B/1338

*9781764219037*